Lucknow Diaries

While **Partha Sarthi Sen Sharma** started writing articles, travel pieces and opinion pieces more than a decade back, which were published in various well-known newspapers and magazines like *The Times of India, Hindustan Times, Swagat, Rail Bandhu, Discover India,* etc., his first full-scale travelogue as a book was published in 2011 as *A Passage across Europe.* In 2015, the author's first novel called *Love Side by Side* hit the stands and since then thousands of readers have read and enjoyed it. His third book, another travelogue covering Britain, Europe, Turkey, Morocco and India, called *Every Mile a Memory* was published in 2016. All of the three books have been translated and published in Hindi too. *Lucknow Diaries: Of Love and Longing,* according to him, is his best creation so far.

Apart from being a writer, Partha Sarthi Sen Sharma is also a full-time civil servant and career bureaucrat, a reader of books, thinker of ideas and a sports and music enthusiast. After living in Lucknow for more than 15 years, he has recently relocated to Delhi, the city where he grew up in. Although he now lives in Delhi, his novel *Lucknow Diaries: Of Love and Longing,* he believes, is his tribute to the city where he spent so many beautiful years.

Lucknow Diaries

OF LOVE AND LONGING

PARTHA SARTHI SEN SHARMA

RUPA

Published by
Rupa Publications India Pvt. Ltd 2018
7/16, Ansari Road, Daryaganj
New Delhi 110002

Sales centres:
Allahabad Bengaluru Chennai
Hyderabad Jaipur Kathmandu
Kolkata Mumbai

ISBN: 978-93-5333-250-1

First impression 2018

10 9 8 7 6 5 4 3 2 1

Printed Nutech Print Services, Faridabad

Looking at the sleepy, quiet streets of Lucknow on that Sunday morning, it was difficult to imagine that barely two months ago the political landscape of the country, and also the state, had changed so suddenly and irreversibly. The young, former prime minister who was also the leader of the grand old party—the one who had promised to take India into the twenty-first century—had been brutally and shockingly assassinated in a remote town in the deep south. Feroze remembered that when he had heard the news flashing across the All India Radio, the first anxious thought that had come to his mind, beyond the initial shock, was about the religious identity of the assassins. It had been the same when the unfortunate mother of the unfortunate son, the then prime minister herself, had been assassinated seven years earlier. It was the same relief when Feroze had learnt that the assassins were not Muslims. Despite that tragedy—or perhaps because of it—the party had managed to recover its position and squeezed in to form a minority government in Delhi, and a veteran politician, who had barely a few months back almost packed up his bags, had found himself at the head of the government and at the helm of tumultuous affairs.

All this had happened miles away from the lazy streets of Hazratganj. Summer vacation had only just started but Lucknow had already turned into a hot cauldron. It was not yet noon and the sun was yet to turn on its full heat. Perhaps because it was Sunday, Hazratganj wore a deserted look. Many of the shopkeepers were enjoying their weekly offs and dark, iron shutters hung over the entrances of the British Book Depot and the Bata showroom opposite. It was still not time for the morning show and so the Capitol and the Mayfair were yet to wake up to excited queues in front of their ticket booths. The only shops that were open, and busy, were the old eateries—Choudhry's, Rovers and, of course, Moti Mahal, where Feroze and his two friends were headed. Instead of their usual bicycles, they were sitting in the old, petrol-guzzling Chevrolet that belonged to Dinesh's father and had clearly seen better days. Dinesh parked the car in one of the bylanes that sprouted from Hazratganj, in front of a freshly whitewashed mansion that belonged to an old Lucknow family. Just like the Chevrolet, the house and its occupants represented an age long gone.

None of the three friends, however, had any interest in their surroundings; they were engrossed in discussing the 'crucial' junctures of the cricket match they had played on the railway ground earlier that morning. They had managed to win a closely fought match against a local team and, although the result of the match itself was inconsequential, the victory was definitely not. Furthermore, Dinesh's performance, both with bat and ball, had been stellar and he was in an exceptionally good mood. But as was his habit, he sidestepped his own performance and focussed on how critical his friends' performances had been to the victory.

'It was your catch that got their captain out and turned the tables on the team. Otherwise, he would have taken the match away from us.' He spoke to Feroze, as they walked towards Moti Mahal.

'Yes, it was spectacular,' affirmed Rahul, the third of the trio and the wicket keeper of the team.

Dusty from their early-morning game, the three friends trooped into the basement eatery, away from the glare of the sun outside. It took a while for their eyes to adjust to the dim interiors but they knew the place like the back of their hands—it was here that they almost always congregated after their Sunday matches. They made their way to their usual corner table. The eatery was noisy, with orders being shouted by the old waiters to the kitchen overhead, but it had loyal clients who came here regularly for the authentic quality of the dishes at prices they could afford. The ambience, or rather the lack of it, didn't bother them at all; the owner, who sat at the till, was aware of that.

The old waiter, Rahim Mian, with his grey stubble and oversized maroon uniform, made his way to the trio as they sat down heavily at their table. There was no question of a printed menu—the old man waited nonchalantly over them, confident that the friends knew what they wanted to order. They always did.

Dinesh ordered for all three of them.

'Rahim Mian, as usual, a dosa for Rahul. Feroze, what will you have?' Dinesh knew it was quite impossible to predict his friend's choice, whether in matters of dishes, shots on the cricket field or anything else in life. As for himself, he used the breather to try and zero in on a dish.

'I think I will try the chhole samosa. I haven't tried that here before,' Feroze replied, squinting at the menu and rate list that had been painted in dirty red on the wall opposite.

'Ok then, Rahim Mian, a dosa for Rahul, a plate of chhole samosa for Feroze and a plate of poori sabzi for me. And, of course, three cups of tea.'

Dinesh remembered that his father had ordered the same years ago, when they had come to this very restaurant as a family for the first time. Raja Surendra Singh, Dinesh's father, was yet to become the famous politician and minister he was now and the family could still enjoy their occasional meals in anonymity at the Hazratganj eateries.

Soon the friends had gone over all the minute points of the morning match and the conversation needed a new topic. There was neither any hurry, nor any need to find a topic of conversation. The day, slowly getting hotter, lay yawning outside and there was not much to do.

Feroze had joined Lucknow University a year back. His course had been decided not so much by his inclination or interest as by the marks he had got in his school final exams. It had also been determined by the fact that his father could not afford to pay the 'donation' that some of the recently opened private engineering colleges, mostly in southern India, demanded. Dinesh had got admission in one of those, against his own wishes but on the insistence of his father. Rahul, on his part, had always been an outstanding student and his marks had got him admission to the local engineering college, as was expected not only by his parents but by everyone else, related or not.

It was a semester break in his college and Dinesh had been able to return to his hometown after almost six months.

'How is Pune as a city?' asked Feroze, squinting at Dinesh as the dishes were laid down in front of them.

'It's nice and green, but Lucknow is Lucknow. There you don't get our kind of food and, of course, there is no Ganjing,' Dinesh replied with a smile, referring to the leisurely strolls down the main thoroughfare of Hazratganj that Lucknowites were so fond of. He didn't want to add that he missed his friends and the affection of his sister in Pune.

Feroze seemed satisfied with the answer. Somehow, he knew he wouldn't have liked it if in Dinesh's estimation, Pune had surpassed Lucknow. Feroze considered himself a true Lucknowite, as his family had lived in the Chowk area of old Lucknow for generations.

'They don't make chaat and kulfi like Ram Asrey does anywhere in Pune,' Dinesh added rather wistfully, referring to the two-century-old famous sweetmeat shop in Lucknow.

'So what is your plan for the day?' Rahul asked no one in particular, as he called for extra coconut chutney and sambhar. He was always thinking ahead.

'Nothing. It is too hot to be outside. I will probably watch a video cassette at home,' Dinesh said. They had bought a colour TV and a video cassette player only a few days back and Dinesh particularly enjoyed watching English movies in the cool darkness of his bedroom. That was his own little den, his cocoon from the heat, dust and noise of the world outside.

'I have my tuitions, of course,' Feroze said. He would cycle from home to distant Indira Nagar and Mahanagar to teach his pupils mathematics, to help them prepare for their board exams.

Rahul himself, however, didn't know what he would have

said if someone had asked him that question. The long, hot summer day stretched before him but he had no plans.

Dinesh paid for all three of them, as was usual, and the friends rose, taking a pinch of fennel and crystal candy before stepping out once again. Hazratganj had slowly begun stirring to life.

The sky was the colour of beaten metal and there was no sign of any cloud. Even the birds had taken refuge somewhere out of sight and a hot wind blew over the dry, deserted streets. Feroze had lived through these hot summer months every year of his life in Lucknow, as there had never been any question of his family being able to afford a summer vacation at a hill station, like some of his more prosperous friends did. And still, at the peak of every summer, his parched soul longed for the cool relief the monsoons would bring. But that was a month away, if one were to believe the predictions of the meteorological department, printed in the Hindi newspapers.

Feroze rode his bicycle past the government medical college named after a long-dead British monarch that continued to hold on to its name even after decades of independence. The original British-era building, all snow white, was a profusion of latticed windows and cupolas that made it appear more like a Rajputana palace than a modern medical college. But still, it was far better, in Feroze's view, than the ugly concrete blocks that had come up haphazardly all over the campus since independence, as successive governments struggled to spare budgets for its expansion.

Feroze pedalled on, despite the heat and the unfavourable slope, past the magnificently built mosque that sat on a mound along the way. The mosque, built by the last great Mughal emperor, was pure white, just like the medical college. He skirted the mosque, past the old government school where he had studied for six long years, and moved on towards the river.

A rare draught of breeze caught his hair as it blew over the still surface of the water. Feroze wanted to stop for a while, not because he was tired but because he wanted to look at the beautiful skyline of the city from the bridge—the city of his forefathers, where generations of his family had been born, had lived and died, and now lay buried—his city, the only one he knew. He could see the sun shining brightly on the metalled umbrella that sat proudly on top of the Chattar Manzil, the great palace of the Nawabs of Awadh that now housed a government research institute. But he didn't dare stop; he was getting late for his tuition class. He still had to cycle a couple of miles to reach the Jains, who lived in the newly developed part of the city, across the Gomti River.

Unlike Feroze, the Jains were not original residents of Lucknow. Mr Jain had arrived only a couple of years ago to pursue his career in the Government of India and was posted in one of the research institutes that had come up in the city after the country's independence. As was usual, Mr Jain was in his office when Feroze reached their house to teach Shreya, a shy teenager struggling with her maths lessons. Feroze, who had been good at Maths in school—far better than Dinesh and almost as good as Rahul—had been approached by Mr Jain through a common acquaintance a couple of months ago. The arrangement did provide Feroze and his family with some extra money but he hoped—and wanted to believe—that his teaching Shreya was more than just a commercial exchange. Although he knew that he needed the money, he didn't want to be reminded of the price tag associated with teaching.

Shreya was a shy, silent and attentive student who always completed her homework and did what she was told. She tried to make up with her patient labour what she lacked in spark or passion. But then, she, along with many girls of her generation, had been brought up in a fashion where duty and responsibility weighed heavy on their young shoulders. Feroze had seen the same in his own family, in the lives of his four sisters, two older than him.

As the cooler tried valiantly to cool the hot drawing room, the class wore on, dull and laborious, as Shreya, guided by Feroze, plodded on through algebraic equations till the hour struck. There had been no small talk, no extraneous conversation between tutor and pupil, even when the manservant of the house brought in the customary tea for Feroze. There was no common ground, experience or interest where the two minds could come together for any conversation—and even if there was, neither ventured to explore it. Shreya's quietness sometimes made Feroze uneasy, as if he were intruding into a sacred space, disturbing something sacrosanct and out of bounds. He hoped that someday Shreya would open up a bit and the situation would become a little more comfortable, a little easier.

Later in the afternoon, after another tuition at the house of the Sahu family, as the sun finally and thankfully started dipping, Feroze stopped on his way back home at the so-called

Company Gardens. He sprawled on the cool grass that carpeted the undulating slopes of the park and looked up at the sky. The Hindi newspapers were full of disturbing news—how some political outfits were talking openly about building a Ram temple at Ayodhya, where a centuries-old mosque stood. The actual dispute itself was not new but it had dragged on in the courts over the years, and somehow, it was only in the recent months that political parties, newspapers and rumour mongers had become interested in it. It disturbed Feroze. He wasn't bothered about which of the two parties was historically right; he was only bothered about the safety and the security of his family, his home and his city. He silently prayed for all of them, as the voice of the muezzin sounded from the tall minarets of the nearby mosque.

Dinesh didn't want to go to Nainital. He would actually have loved to escape the now scorching heat of Lucknow but he didn't want to accompany his sibling, cousins, uncle and aunt, who were planning to go in a large group to the hill station. They had already booked a number of rooms in a hotel overlooking the lake, situated right on the touristy Mall Road. Dinesh still remembered the time, long ago in his childhood, when his father would take him, his mother and his sister on the occasional summer vacation to Nainital. His mother would sit for long hours on the balcony of their hotel room, looking out at the mist hovering over the surface of the lake, its colour changing with the quality of the sunlight that fell on it. She loved nature, open spaces and the quiet solitude they brought, but these were the very things that were denied to her in her husband's large joint family, where the responsibilities of her in-laws, her husband's younger siblings and his extended family kept her busy.

This was before Dinesh's father decided to join politics. Raja Saheb, as he was called by the multitudes who had voted for him, had, since then, become an important minister in the provincial government of the state and nursed yet higher ambitions, although in public he denied them. Dinesh, of course, knew better than to believe what he publicly claimed.

'Why don't you come along too? It will be fun, and it is so hot here! I remember how you used to enjoy the long walks in the hills when we went there as children.' Dinesh's train of thought was interrupted by this sudden remark from Amrita, his younger sister, who, unknown to Dinesh, had come out of the house to where he was sitting on a wicker chair in the long, covered verandah.

'You go. I am sure you'll all enjoy very much.' Dinesh didn't say whether he would go. He knew that he could not explain to Amrita his real reasons for refusing to accompany them to the hills. It was partly because he himself didn't understand them. How could he explain to her that he longed for distance from his own family, or that he felt he would tire of listening to the incessant small talk of his cousins and aunt—or that he would painfully be reminded of childhood vacations when their mother was still with them and their father had not drifted away to public life.

Amrita sat down silently on a chair beside her elder brother. Only a couple of years separated them but, lately, especially since

Dinesh had left home for college a year ago, the distance and the difference between them seemed to have widened. Sometimes Amrita longed for her brother of old, who shared his thoughts and feelings, his doubts and ambitions with her; who saved his precious little pocket money to buy her Cadbury's Dairy Milk chocolates, which they would eventually eat together.

She followed Dinesh's gaze towards the manicured lawns, part of the government bungalow that had been allotted to their father as a Cabinet minister. The sun was setting and had lost much of its heat. Though it was still warm, the whirring overhead fan was sufficient. A peacock had appeared from somewhere and was now sitting on the boundary wall of the bungalow. The fleeting rays of the setting sun rippled on its glistening blue neck, as it turned its head this way and that to survey its surroundings. The gardener, dark and sinewy, was watering the flower beds and lawns. Dinesh had been watching the gardener come everyday to work on the lawns silently and laboriously, season after season, year after year, but realized that he didn't even know his name. The beauty of the flowerbeds and the well-kept lawns was the only proof of his existence.

'Ramdeen really loves his work. It is perhaps this that makes the plants and flowers so beautiful,' Amrita observed.

She had been trying to follow her brother's line of sight and, with it, his thoughts. Dinesh was surprised that Amrita knew the gardener's name. But then she had always had that rare empathy for people that Dinesh felt was missing in him. It was not that he lacked concern, especially for those from the lower strata of society, but it was always in a rather distant, abstract and theoretical manner that he thought of them.

He would read and talk about class struggles but had never thought of talking to the gardener whom he saw everyday. It was a quality that he shared with his father, who, in his youth, had joined the communist party, only to be disillusioned a couple of years later. Amrita had inherited her 'human connect' from their mother, as also her classic looks. Dinesh only hoped that his loving, sensitive sister would not inherit their mother's lonely and sad life as well.

Monsoons finally arrived in Lucknow and the sky was a huge mass of rolling, heaving grey clouds. Rahul was sitting on the terrace of his house, looking at the sky and thinking of nothing in particular. It was a weekend and time lay heavy on him. It was one of those days when, despite everything being perfectly normal, he felt a strange inexplicable restlessness inside him. His life, for all practical purposes, was on an even keel. He was studying in a well-known government engineering college and had a well-defined career ahead of him. He should not have too much problem in getting a decent-salaried job once he got out of college a few years on. And yet Rahul was consumed by an inner dissatisfaction, as if he were still looking for some yet-unknown course of life. It was a feeling that he could not articulate in words or share with his friends and family.

It had rained in the morning and the floor of the terrace was still wet in patches, creating strange and ever-changing patterns as the puddles gradually evaporated. A bulbul had perched itself on the cord that ran diagonally across the terrace, and was used to dry clothes. There were earthen flower pots arranged along the edge of the terrace, proof of the green fingers of his parents. Rahul had not yet decided what to do with the day that stretched before him. Maybe he would go and meet Dinesh or Feroze. He knew he only needed a couple of hours to prepare for his weekly Monday test in college. Or he could just lie in bed, watching cricket on TV, lazing. Both prospects were nice but not enthralling. It seemed to uncannily mirror his life. The very thought depressed him.

Rahul loved the terrace more than any other place in the house. It gave him a sense of space, light and freedom that eluded him in the two cramped rooms of their government-allotted house. Rahul's father worked as a junior officer in the State Electricity Board, having recently been promoted after years of drudgery as an accountant. It was a Sunday, and Rahul's father was sitting on his usual chair in the so-called living room, reading newspapers and ordering endless cups of tea. It was an unchanging, unending pattern that played out every Sunday in their house. As was usual, Rahul's mother was in the small, dark kitchen, busy cooking their next meal. Rahul could occasionally hear sounds coming from that direction—utensils clanking or the hiss of chopped vegetables being released in hot oil.

Rahul viewed his parents' lives as even more monotonous than his own, with no hope of any change in future. He wondered if they ever noticed the despondent monotony of their lives that seemed so depressingly boring to his youthful and restless mind.

Rahul got up from his solitary stupor and decided to go for a haircut, not because he felt that his hair needed cutting but only so he could escape the sheer boredom of the day.

He announced to his mother from the kitchen entrance: 'I am going to get a haircut.'

'Ok, but try to be back in time for lunch. Your father would not like to be kept waiting.'

The morning rain had left puddles on the footpath, but having grown up in these very environs, neither the puddles, nor the hawkers sitting on the footpath selling combs and sunglasses bothered Rahul. He dodged the puddles, hawkers, the occasional biker riding on the footpath, and the stray cow that seemed to have lost its way, to reach the barber's shop. The shop was named after a long-forgotten and long-departed English gentleman, whose descendants now probably lived in some faraway English countryside, ignorant of their family name still being used at the entrance of a barber shop miles away, across oceans, in a city that they had never seen. The present owners of the shop were equally oblivious to its history and heritage, and the hand-painted name on the tin signboard was the only indication of the forgotten age in which it was first used.

It was only when Rahul stepped inside the shop that he realized what was amiss since morning. The voice of Sushil Doshi drifted from the radio and he realized he had forgotten about the test match that had started earlier in the day. It was after quite a few years that Lucknow was hosting an international match, which was being played barely a couple of miles down the barber shop, at the other end of Hazratganj. Rahul remembered that Dinesh's father, a minister, had been offered complimentary passes by the organizers and that Dinesh had chosen Feroze over Rahul to accompany him. It had rankled with Rahul, despite knowing that Feroze was more interested in cricket than him and also that it would be much more difficult for Feroze to afford the tickets. Of course, there was no question of Dinesh asking his father for an additional pass.

As Shakeel, the barber, started on his hair, Rahul closed his eyes, having finally ascertained the cause of his uneasiness.

Results of the final-year examinations of Feroze's Composite History course at Lucknow University were to be announced that day. Rakesh, his friend and classmate, had come over to Feroze's house and was waiting in the verandah of the ancestral house as Feroze got ready. Stray green weeds had come up through gaps between the ancient stones that paved the courtyard and a small peepul sapling had raised its head from a crevice in the wall. Although Feroze's family was Muslim, Rakesh knew that the peepul tree, sacred to Hindus, would not be uprooted.

The results were supposed to have been announced a few weeks back but due to some reason unfathomable to the students, they had been delayed. Feroze didn't have high expectations. He knew he would pass with reasonably respectable marks, like so many others from similar courses in similar universities across India. He knew that the degree didn't give him any assurance, much less a guarantee, of a career or a livelihood. That is why, while waiting for the results, he had started working part time at the editorial office of an Urdu newspaper, *Inquilaab*. Although he was a Muslim, he didn't know how to read or write the Persian script. So he wrote his copies in English, his second language after Hindi, which were then translated by the two professional Urdu scribes at the paper who were paid to translate newscopies and agency feed that poured in everyday. He would be going to the office of *Inquilaab* in the afternoon, after the results were out.

Feroze put on a clean, white cotton kurta over his old pair of jeans, combed his wet hair and came out into the courtyard. He hadn't shaved, as he didn't want to keep Rakesh waiting. He didn't bother to announce to his family—his mother and sisters—that he was going to get his results. It was not that he had any particular reason not to do so; the thought had just never occurred to him.

As Feroze and Rakesh rode into the sprawling university campus on their black Hercules bicycles, Feroze thought about how this could be the last time he ever entered the portals of the university, at least as a student. He had been an ardent student and had loved his classes, especially those taken by Ms Basu, the lecturer of Contemporary Indian History. It was Ms Basu, with her enthusiasm and erudition, who had opened up Feroze's mind to how history, especially contemporary history, has the power to affect the present and how its pulse beats through everyday events, only if somebody has the ears to hear it.

Ms Basu was particularly fond of Feroze and never made any effort to conceal her feelings. It was something that Feroze's friends, including Rakesh, took every opportunity to tease him about. That Ms Basu was slim, good-looking and a divorcee only added to their jokes, but Feroze knew, or rather liked to believe, that Ms Basu's interest in him was purely academic and that it was his friends' own suppressed proclivities that distorted the liberal and frank overtures of his teacher.

Ms Basu wanted Feroze to continue his studies and join the MA course. Although Feroze would have liked to, he knew that was not to be. His proud father would never admit, even to himself, that it would help if Feroze started earning as soon as possible—but Feroze knew he had a duty as a son and a brother.

As they reached their department, they could see a group of students huddled in front of the noticeboard, where huge, white, type-written sheets of paper announcing their marks had been pasted. Feroze recognized, even from a distance, three of them—Lata, Manoj and Vikram. As they approached the noticeboard, Feroze knew, even without looking, that Rakesh was silently muttering prayers. Rakesh, who belonged to a family from the mofussil area, had come to Lucknow three years ago to join the university. Although he had no clear picture in his mind about what he wanted to do in his life and how his marks would help him do that—like so many of his fellow students—he had been brought up to believe that every single mark of every single exam was important and would somehow pave the way to a golden future.

It turned out that Feroze had scored better than he had expected. Although he had not topped—that was reserved for Lata—he knew Ms Basu would be pleased, but also very disappointed that he would not be studying further. Their last meeting had turned bitter, as Ms Basu couldn't understand why Feroze was being so obstinate, refusing to even fill in the admission forms for the MA course.

'Congratulations, Feroze, you really have got very good marks.' It was Lata. Feroze couldn't help observing that Lata was, for the first time, wearing a sari to university. The deep green cotton sari made her look like a woman rather than the young girl he remembered from class. He observed, too, that Lata was expecting to be complimented on her own marks.

'Congratulations to you! You were always the topper, and today, too, you are head and shoulders above all of us.' Feroze genuinely complimented Lata.

'Why don't we go over and thank Ms Basu for all she has done for us?'

Feroze was not sure whether Lata meant going with all the other students of their class as well. However, he soon found out, as only the two of them walked up the stairs to the first floor, where Ms Basu had her room. Feroze felt a sense of gratitude towards Ms Basu that had nothing to do with his recently acquired marks. But verbal expressions of gratitude, or other such feelings, didn't come naturally to him. So, in a way, he was glad that Lata was with him.

Thankfully, Ms Basu was present in her room, peering over some papers stacked on her small table. Sunlight coming in through the open window was the only source of illumination, as there seemed to be 'load-shedding'—as all electricity disruptions were described in common parlance.

'Oh, hi! Congratulations to both of you.' Ms Basu looked up from her table, putting her reading glasses away, as Feroze and Lata entered her tiny room. Feroze was sure Ms Basu was aware of the results but whether she was already expecting them or surprised to find them in her room he couldn't say.

'Madam, we wanted to thank you for teaching us and making the subject so interesting. Without you, we wouldn't have got the marks we did.' Lata was politeness personified.

'Thank you,' Ms Basu replied, shifting slightly to look at them. 'You know, I feel both happy and sad at the same time. I feel happy looking at your achievements, your marks and your happiness, but also sad that my students will now be leaving us.'

Feroze knew that Lata had already got admission in the School of Oriental and African Studies in London and would soon be flying out to pursue her higher studies. He felt a pang of remorse and unexpected self-pity at the thought of Lata pursuing her cherished dreams of higher academics while he was held back in this city, unable even to pursue his post-graduation at Lucknow University.

'Feroze, I know you won't agree with me but I really feel you should continue with your post-graduation, even if through evening classes or correspondence. You have a genuine appreciation of history, as few have, and a way of looking at and expressing historic events that is uniquely your own. I know we have gone through this conversation before but if I can ever change your mind or be of any help, please feel free to ring me up.' Ms Basu scribbled her mobile number on a small slip of paper and gave it to an astonished Feroze. She was one of the first few in the university to have acquired a mobile phone—a heavy, black Motorola handset that she took with her wherever she went.

Feroze hardly ever gave in to impulses but today he surprised even himself as he said, 'Madam, you might just have changed my mind. I think I will indeed enrol myself on the university correspondence course to do my post-graduation. I know it may not be the same and that I will miss your classes but I guess something is better than nothing.' It was as if somebody else had entered his body and was speaking through him. Before that moment, he had given no thought to a correspondence course but now that he had said it aloud to a visibly pleased Ms Basu, he couldn't bring himself to disappoint her.

It was the last semester break before the end of the four-year engineering course. The campus wore a deserted look, as most of the students and faculty had gone home. The classrooms, the playing fields, the canteen and the staff rooms were all silent and empty. But Dinesh had preferred to stay back. He was not sure what had led to that decision—it was one of those instinctive, impulsive decisions that he would rationalize later. He knew his father was once again contesting to retain his constituency and seat in the legislative assembly of the state, and was busy campaigning for the elections. But then, he thought, his father was always busy. Since he had joined politics, and especially since Dinesh's mother's death, father and son had grown distant. Dinesh knew Amrita would have been looking forward to his visit home and would not only be disappointed but also worried about him. But still, Dinesh wanted to spend his last semester break away from home.

Dinesh was, however, not alone and three of his friends—Ajay, Gautam and Rajesh—had also stayed back at the hostel with him. Bala, a day scholar and a local resident, had invited the friends to the occasional home-cooked meal, but for other days, although the hostel mess was officially closed, the friends had pooled in money and paid the contractual mess workers to prepare meals for them.

However, in his heart of hearts, Dinesh knew he had stayed back for Geeta Zutshi, the only girl in their Mechanical Engineering class. She had also decided to stay back this last semester break and was now the sole occupant of the girls' hostel that stood across the playfield, opposite to where Dinesh was standing that morning, sipping his cup of tea. Dinesh knew that for three years, Dinesh and Geeta had shared the same course, attended the same workshops, exchanged pleasantries and even shared the occasional banter, but the relationship between them, if he could dare call it that, had never progressed beyond the strict boundaries of accepted norms. He, however, was always acutely conscious of the attraction he felt towards her. Now that the course was drawing to an inevitable end, he hoped for some providential event, some chance, for the ice to break.

Suddenly, as if by the sheer power of his concealed yearnings, he saw Geeta walking across the playfield, straight towards their hostel. It was such a striking coincidence that it appeared unreal to Dinesh. But Geeta was indeed coming towards him, confident in her stride and apparently looking at him too—although it was impossible to tell from a distance. She seemed to be wearing riding boots and breeches—perhaps she had been to the riding ground behind the girls' hostel. A few students took horse-riding classes there at special concessional rates; Dinesh had heard Geeta was one of them and also probably the reason for many other students to enrol.

'Hi, how are you this morning?' Geeta had reached Dinesh

while he was lost in thought and was now standing opposite him. Dinesh could see tiny droplets of perspiration on her temple and a few wet strands of hair on her fair forehead.

'I am fine. And you? I didn't know you were staying back too during the break,' Dinesh lied, which he immediately realized was quite unintentional and wholly unnecessary.

'I am fine too but a bit bored, as I am the only girl left in the hostel,' Geeta replied. 'Listen, I have come here to ask for a favour. It is getting impossible for me to manage my meals all alone there. Can I join in your mess arrangements here and come here during mealtimes? I would, of course, pay my share. It would really save me a lot of hassle; I never thought cooking could be such a chore,' Geeta asked, looking straight at him.

Dinesh knew he ought to consult his friends with whom he shared the mess arrangements, but he also knew that he couldn't wait for such consultations, not now, and he anyway knew what the outcome would be.

'Yes, of course. Not an issue at all,' he replied, putting on his most nonchalant face, fervently hoping the elation he felt inside wouldn't show.

Geeta was an exceptionally beautiful girl—only a blind person would fail to see that—but that morning, Dinesh felt, she looked especially radiant, her beauty lighting up everything around.

'Ok, then, from this lunch on, I will come over for the meals. I will pay for the arrangements when I come this afternoon.' It appeared to Dinesh that Geeta was being very particular not to take any favour from anyone, eager to keep things straight and simple, without the burden of obligations and expectations.

It was only when Geeta had started walking back towards her hostel that Dinesh realized how uncouth it had been of him not to have offered her a cup of tea, while standing there the whole time with his own cup in his hand.

Rahul was at a loose end. Quite inexplicably, Dinesh had preferred to stay back for the semester break and Feroze was busy balancing his taxing job as a reporter for the Urdu newspaper and his evening post-graduation classes, which he had switched to from the initial correspondence course. Rahul realized how much he had been looking forward to Dinesh's arrival, and his absence seemed to create a vacuum in his own vacation that was getting increasingly difficult to fill.

He had come out, all alone, to the sprawling Lohia Park in the heart of the city, which had been inaugurated just a few days ago. It was a nice, open piece of land, but he had come there not so much to enjoy the landscape as to escape his shared Sunday at home with his father. It was only half an hour back that his conversation with his father had turned uneasy, if not unpleasant. As was usual, it revolved around Rahul's future and his career plans.

'So what have you decided for your future, if at all?' It was his father, Arun Srivastava, who had started the conversation. His gesture of neatly folding up the newspaper earlier than usual in the morning was a sign that he had decided to have a longish and, to his mind, meaningful discussion with his son.

'Some companies will be coming to the college for campus

recruitment in the final semester,' Rahul had replied. He intended to start earning as soon as possible.

'But why not go for an MTech degree? It is always advisable to get as many educational qualifications as possible. Otherwise, later in life, it may turn out to be a handicap, as I have found out in my own,' Mr Srivastava said. Rahul knew that his father had been forced to abort his own studies due to the precarious financial condition of his family. They had earlier lived in the industrial township of Kanpur, where Rahul's grandfather had worked in an old textile factory set up almost a century ago with British capital but which had long since outlived its useful years. The inevitable technological obsolescence, coupled with labour strikes and lockouts, had resulted in the factory closing down at a time that coincided with his father's school final examinations. As a result, despite brilliant marks, he had been forced to start working as a lowly clerk as the sole earning member of the family, and his dream of getting admission into Harcourt Butler Technical Institute had never been realised. It was this untimely abortion of a promising career that had always rankled with Mr Srivastava. Perhaps it was his deep-seated frustration, long forgotten by others, that had turned Rahul's father bitter.

'The best jobs are being offered to fresh engineering graduates, and only those who are not getting jobs are enrolling on the MTech course,' Rahul defended his decision. It was indeed true, but the real reason Rahul didn't want to do MTech was because he was really not interested in Engineering. He had enrolled on the course only because it offered a relatively secure career and job prospects. And it was the only logical and acceptable course to follow, given his high marks and subject combination in the school final exams. But Rahul knew his relationship with his father would not be able to withstand the deep truth of his choice; it was better to skim the surface.

'You are fortunate that you have the luxury of going for a post-graduate course. Not many have that. I do not want you to regret later in your career, when such an opportunity will no longer be available.' Mr Srivastava insisted on continuing his line of reasoning.

Rahul knew that some of what his father said made conventional sense. But he had come to realize, during his Engineering course, that a career in this field would feed his body but not his soul. Instead, he had secretly started harbouring an ambition to join the civil services and had even started to collect study material for the tough entrance exams. However, he didn't feel confident enough yet to divulge his ambitions to the outside world. And his own father, he realized, belonged to that world.

It was the busiest Feroze had ever been, but, for once, he was enjoying every bit of it. He had decided to work as a field reporter for *Inquilaab* during the day and as a desk editor at night. The newspaper, like most Urdu newspapers, was not financially strong, as it did not have the backing of any big business group. It was all the more reason why it appreciated Feroze doubling as a reporter and an assistant editor. On his part, Feroze loved getting out into the thick of things, covering events, listening to people, interviewing them and soaking in experiences, sometimes historic. When time permitted, he would try to attend the evening post-graduation classes, especially those of History, when Ms Basu would lecture on the contemporary world and Indian history. He loved connecting the dots as he sat through her classes, the dots of past and present, separated by ages and miles, across centuries and continents.

Although Feroze liked working for the newspaper, its owners and especially its old-school editor, he had applied for the post of assistant editor with a leading English daily that was planning to open its bureau office in Lucknow. For one, the salary was better and, for another, Feroze wanted to see his own words in print, not the result of a translation undecipherable to him. He knew that more than a hundred candidates had applied for the posts on offer and that his chances were admittedly slim, mainly due to his lack of experience. This was why the exclusive interview that Feroze was about to take that day of Raja Surendra Singh, revenue minister in the Uttar Pradesh government, was especially important. He secretly hoped that his prospective employers would notice the interview, even if it was in Urdu.

Feroze was not sure whether Raja Saheb was doing his son's friend a favour by agreeing to give him the interview. However, even if he did, he didn't show any of it and treated Feroze with a courtesy that would have been more suited for a seasoned editor.

'Sir, first of all, let me thank you for agreeing to give this interview to our small newspaper.' Feroze started the interview with the usual warm-up statement, as he had seen his senior editor do in similar circumstances.

'Not at all, it is entirely my pleasure.' Raja Saheb was correctness personified.

'Sir, you are seeking re-election from the electorate after

having served as a Cabinet minister in the government for five years. What will you go to the voters with this time?' Feroze asked, ready to write down the answer.

'I think our government, under the able and dynamic leadership of our Chief Minister, has done a lot for all sections of people, especially the poor and the oppressed. We will go to the elections with the record of our work and ask for votes based on our performance.' Again, Raja Saheb was politically correct.

'Who do you think is your biggest political opponent in this election?' This was one of the questions Feroze had discussed the previous day with his editor, Hisam Saheb, who had been a bit surprised to learn that Raja Surendra Singh, the virtual No 2 in the government, had agreed to grant Feroze, a newcomer, an exclusive interview.

'I think we really do not have any serious challenger, but if you insist, we would like to name communal forces as our real opponent.'

Feroze knew that the politician was addressing Lucknow's sizeable Muslim population, especially as Feroze represented an Urdu newspaper. The interview was so far moving on entirely predictable lines and Feroze was desperately looking for a response, a remark that could be turned into a headline and make the front page. He didn't know that Raja Saheb, too, was looking for the same.

'Sir, are you in the race to become chief minister, if your party comes back to power?' Feroze was now treading on dangerous, tricky areas, trying to get a newsworthy response.

'I have complete faith in our Chief Minister, our leader. However, I am ready to shoulder any responsibility that the party high command may trust me with.' Once again, Raja Surendra Singh had said the correct thing, but in that fleeting moment, with an exchange of glances, both knew that the penny had dropped—the headline had been made. 'Raja Surendra Singh declares himself a contender for the chief minister's post.' A headline that would be denied by Raja Saheb, of course, and yet remain the talk of the town, and the state, for days to come. For both of them, the interview had served its purpose. Raja Saheb had indeed done Feroze a favour.

Dinesh couldn't figure out why Geeta, the most beautiful girl in college, had 'chosen' him. Left to himself, he wouldn't have dared to imagine this but the constant teasing by his friends made him think that way. He had to admit that Geeta did indeed seem to spend most of her time with him—in the classroom, at workshops and laboratories, and even outside of them. It had all started that morning when Geeta had walked across the playfield that separated their hostels. And now it had almost been a year and the final examinations were coming to an end. Between trying to mug up notes from his classmate and topper Anuj, Dinesh wondered what lay in store for him after college. The month-long industrial training the previous year had bored him to death and made it amply clear that an engineering job was not for him. Moreover, he knew his father would not like his only son to do a routine nine-to-five job. Raja Surendra Singh had won the re-election and become the deputy chief minister of the state government.

However, the wily Chief Minister Vibhuti Narayan Pandey, while apparently giving him a promotion, had taken away all the important portfolios from him and reduced his powers to grant patronages and favours. Although Dinesh stayed miles away from Lucknow and its politics, Lucknow never quite stayed away from him.

At college, only Geeta knew of Dinesh's father's political position, because her own was a senior engineer in the state Public Works Department. Mr Zutshi had recently been transferred from a provincial district headquarters to Lucknow on a promotion and Dinesh couldn't help thinking about how, once their engineering course was over, Geeta could be living in Lucknow, maybe even closer to his father's official bungalow than her hostel was to his now.

If Dinesh's father's political position made any difference to Geeta, it didn't show in her behaviour. In fact, she was the most carefree human being Dinesh had ever met. Dinesh particularly admired her rare quality to live in the moment—a quality he constantly, and unsuccessfully, tried to imbibe.

'Do you realize that a chapter in our lives is coming to an end? It will never be the same again once we leave college.' Dinesh remarked, looking at Geeta. They were in Dinesh's hostel room that afternoon, preparing for their last examination on Dynamics of Machines. 'We will all go our separate ways after this.' The rays of the afternoon sun were sneaking through the flimsy curtains of the room and playing with Geeta's hair, unknown to her.

'Yes, but then who knows what paths our futures will hold?' Geeta glanced up from her book. 'We are moving from a phase of relative certainty to one of uncertainty.'

'Have you thought of what you want to do with your life?' Of all the time they had spent together, this was the first time they were discussing anything remotely to do with their future. Maybe, somehow unconsciously, they had always pushed such questions away.

There was a pause and then Geeta replied, 'I do not know, at least not yet. But I do know what I don't want to do with my life. I do not want to go into a government job—I have seen my father spending his life in one. And I do not want to do an engineering job. It does not really interest me and I do not think I will be any good at it either. I am still looking for my calling, I suppose.'

Dinesh knew that being a girl, and the girl she was, Geeta could dare to postpone, albeit for a while, decisions about her career and life—a luxury that was denied to most of their college mates. The rest of the students were already under intense pressure from their families, and from society in general, to immediately start pursuing a job, a career and to 'settle down'. Many of them had started appearing for job interviews; a lucky few had even landed jobs as trainee engineers.

As for Dinesh, he had not applied anywhere. Not only did the prospect of a boring nine-to-five job put him off, but Dinesh, unbeknown to himself, also feared rejection.

The sun had lost much of its heat by now and Dinesh had just started to yearn for a cup of tea when there was a knock on the door, which had deliberately been kept ajar. Bala had a strange expression on his face as he stepped in.

'Dinesh, my father just heard on the radio news bulletin,' Bala blurted out. While he had rushed to Dinesh's room, he had been thinking about how to break the news to his friend, but when the moment actually arrived, he found himself unable to temper his speech and just blurted out.

'Dinesh, your father has met with a terrible accident. His helicopter crashed while he was on a tour. The news came in the afternoon bulletin on radio.'

Bala moved closer and put an arm around his friend.

For a second, Dinesh didn't know how to react. The only fervent question in his mind was whether his father was alive—and if so, how and where he was.

'My father couldn't tell. It was a very brief mention.' Bala said, anticipating the silent query that had formed on Dinesh's lips.

'Let me go to the STD booth and ring up home.' Dinesh realized he was more composed than he felt. His anxiety had overtaken any possible grief, at least for the moment. Both Bala and Geeta, in shocked silence, walked Dinesh to the tiny glass cubicle that stood at the college's reception.

Childhood memories and Amrita's face came up before Dinesh's misty eyes as he dialled home and heard the telephone ring. But it was his aunt, not Amrita, who answered.

'Thank God, Dinesh, you called! We were so anxious to reach you. Bhaiyyaji has met with a terrible accident.'

'Is he alive?'

'Yes, yes. Thank God for that. He is critically injured but alive.' Unknown to Dinesh, she had deliberately stopped herself from adding 'still' to the sentence. Luckily, the accident had happened just after the helicopter had taken off at the Lucknow airport and Raja Saheb could be quickly brought to the medical college. Dinesh could barely make out what his aunt was trying to say, her incoherent sentences punctuated by gasps and sobs.

It was the first time Dinesh travelled by air, taking an Air India flight first from Pune to Delhi and then from Delhi to Lucknow. As the plane flew over white clouds, Dinesh's mind was shrouded by a hazy numbness. Although he had always being agnostic, like his father, he found a prayer on his lips. He wanted his father to live, at whatever cost. It was as if, despite all the years of distance and differences, the filial cord between them had suddenly come to life.

There was a huge crowd assembled at the gate of the trauma centre at the medical college. There were media persons, party workers, old friends and supporters, people who had worked with or known Raja Saheb over the years, or simply onlookers who were curious to see what the crowd was about. There were policemen too. Dinesh pushed through the crowd, desperately trying to identify himself, until a local politician recognized him and ushered him through the security cordons and closed gates to the ICU.

The contrast between the noise outside and the eerie silence of the ICU was stark. The heavily bandaged body of Dinesh's father was lying on a white hospital bed, connected to a number of tubes and instruments, unconscious. The only sound was the soft hum of the air conditioner, as a nurse silently moved around the room, checking the tubes, monitors and medicines. There were two other people in the room, sitting on chairs beside his father's bed. One was his sister Amrita, who looked up at the sound of Dinesh's entry, and the other an old man sitting with his back to the door whom Dinesh did not instantly recognize.

Dinesh's first instinct was to rush to his father and embrace him, but the profusion of tubes and pipes attached to his body made that impossible. Instead, brother and sister clung to each other, drawing comfort from each other's presence in that moment of shared shock and sorrow. No words needed to be spoken.

It was a few minutes before Dinesh realized that the man sitting hunched beside his father's bed was none other than the Chief Minister of Uttar Pradesh, Vibhuti Narayan Pandey. Pandeyji, the old, yet powerful man who had served the largest state of India for years and was one of the last of a generation of politicians that had taken active part in India's freedom struggle, was looking at the face of the man who was his colleague, his comrade, his deputy and his friend.

'Dinesh, I have already spoken to the doctors. Whatever can humanly be done is being done. No effort is being spared, I assure you.' Pandeyji had stood up and was speaking to Dinesh in a soft, halting, yet warm voice. 'I think—I hope—he survives, but how much he will recover no one can say. You are his son and you have to be strong at this critical juncture. I am always there and you can directly get in touch with me any time and for anything you want. I was, in fact, waiting only for you.'

Pandeyji gave Dinesh his direct phone number, which was never made public. At any other time, Dinesh would have felt overwhelmed, but at that moment, all he could think of was the old, helpless man on the hospital bed and his sister, sobbing softly in his arms.

Feroze had got the job. Since he had joined the newly opened bureau office of the *Times of Hindustan* in Lucknow, he had become somewhat financially comfortable. Although he would dutifully hand over his entire salary to his mother every month, he would take back a small amount as 'pocket money' for his few needs and indulgences. One such indulgence was enjoying the occasional tobacco-less paan—the peculiarly Indian concoction of spices and condiments wrapped neatly inside betel leaves. Usually, deep into the night, on his way home from work, he would stop at Awasthiji's paan shop. After a hectic day as a staff reporter at the severely understaffed office, it would be the first time during the day that Feroze would take a deep breath and review his day, his life and the world around him. Usually, he would be one of the last customers at the shop, when the old man would be going through his closing ritual of matching the day's accounts and the stock, putting the spices, condiments and betel leaves in their proper containers, and wrapping up for the day. Despite being separated by age, class, religion and education, Feroze and Awasthiji would chat about almost everything under the sun. Feroze liked to believe it gave him the opportunity to understand society better and to pick up any news that might be slipping under the radar of mainstream media. And indeed, on more than one occasion, this hole-in-the-wall shop had given him valuable clues and subtext to events happening around him. It was equidistant from both the Press Club at Chinagate and the Darulshafa, the residence of members of state legislature, and therefore frequented by members of both.

Today, despite it being Feroze's weekly off, he had walked up to office as a matter of routine. Since the election, all news seemed to have dried up and it was getting increasingly difficult to fill up the pages of the newspaper and the appetite of the readers. He had, in his desperate search for news, walked up in the hot afternoon to Awasthiji's shop. He was waiting for his turn to be served, when he saw their office peon, Mangeram, cycling furiously towards him. Feroze wondered how Mangeram knew where to find him.

'Sir, Mr Ghosh has called you urgently to office?' Mangeram had a peculiar habit of turning every sentence into a question, as if he himself was not sure of what he was saying and needed affirmation to rest his doubts.

'Why? Today is my weekly off. I had just come to office; I didn't have any specific work.' Feroze said more to himself than to Mangeram. He knew the poor peon would not know why the resident editor had called his staff reporter so urgently.

It was Mr Ghosh who had made Feroze's transition from the obscure Urdu newspaper to India's largest English daily so smooth. Feroze would not claim that Mr Ghosh had been especially kind to him but he had been fair in his dealings—and that was something Feroze valued, as he had found it so rarely in his life. It was Mr Ghosh who had assigned Feroze to cover Raja Surendra Singh's re-election campaign, perhaps prompted by his interview that had started it all. Feroze had accompanied Raja Saheb whenever the latter agreed, on numerous campaign trails in white ambassador cars, on all kind of roads to distant villages and mofussil towns of rural Uttar Pradesh. Having been born and brought up in the city, it was Feroze's first foray into the thick and thin of real India, to places that had so far only been dots on the map to him—Gonda, Basti, Mau, Lalitpur.

On a couple of occasions, Raja Saheb had even taken Feroze with him on his helicopter, much to the chagrin of some senior journalists.

And today again, it was Raja Saheb who had caused Mr Ghosh to summon Feroze to office so urgently.

'Raja Surendra Singh has met with an accident. The news just came in. Apparently, his helicopter crashed on the airstrip at Lucknow airport.'

The news came as a bolt to Feroze. His first thought was of Dinesh. Where was he? Did he know? How would he react to the news? Who would give him strength and comfort? Only then did his newly acquired journalistic instincts kick in.

'When did this happen? How and where is he?'

'He is being brought to the medical college.' Mr Ghosh didn't have to tell him any more; Feroze was already on his way to the recently inaugurated trauma centre at the old medical college building.

The crowd at the gate of the trauma centre was still small when Feroze reached. The district magistrate and the senior superintendent of police were already there, so also was the principal of the medical college, Dr Varshney. The ambulance carrying Raja Saheb and the pilot of the helicopter was expected any moment now. Feroze couldn't find any of his ilk but was sure they would all turn up soon enough. He went up to the SSP, whom he knew from his days at *Inquilaab*.

'Hello, sir.'

The SSP, Tarun Kumar, didn't smile as he acknowledged Feroze—the situation didn't warrant pleasantries. There was a curious mix of shock, anxiety and sorrow on his face.

'How did this happen, sir?'

'Too early to say anything for sure. Seems to be a technical snag. Of course, a thorough enquiry will be set up.' The SSP looked at the gate of the trauma centre, where the crowd was building up.

Suddenly, the air was filled with the sound of screaming sirens, as a deep blue Gypsy escorting a white ambulance entered through the gates. Everyone—the doctors, the policemen, the nurses and the ward boys, even the casual onlookers—was filled with a nervous energy, all moving at once. Feroze just about managed to get a glimpse of the two bodies, bleeding and burnt, as they were rushed on stretchers to the lift that would take them to the ICU. From the mad rush of the hospital staff, it was clear that they were not dead, at least not yet. That in itself was a matter of great relief to Feroze.

Later that day, as Feroze typed out his news story, certain that Raja Surendra Singh would live despite the terrible accident, Dinesh managed to push past the crowds and the security, and caught the first glimpse of his father on the white hospital bed.

Ever since he was a child, there was a deep-seated desire in Rahul to be admired and praised, which had perhaps been the strongest subconscious motivation for him to excel at studies. Rahul's desire for accolades, coupled with a need to be useful to society and country, had nudged him towards the civil service exams.

After he had passed the final semester exams with high marks, Rahul had, out of a sense of deference to his father's wishes, enrolled on an MTech course in his own engineering college. But all his energy, attention and effort were directed at the civil service exams. To Rahul's relief, his father, for once, had not only agreed with his decision but also supported it. Rahul had overheard his father telling his mother how proud he was of his son's decision to compete for the civil services and his courage to aim high.

Dinesh had, after passing his final-year exams, returned to Lucknow. It was clear to everybody that destiny was pushing him towards a life in politics. Raja Saheb had, for more than a year now, been confined to his bed, almost in a state of coma, hanging between life and death. That one incident, Rahul saw, had scarred his friend from the inside. Although Dinesh behaved normally with everyone, it was obvious that his father's constant suffering, coupled with the silent burden of the family's present and future, lay heavy on his shoulders.

Whenever Rahul and Feroze met—and Rahul made sure they met at least once a week—they shared their concern for Dinesh, who was always present through his absence.

Rahul and Feroze had that day decided to meet up at the brand-new café that had recently opened in Hazratganj. With its bright orange interiors and its neat young staff in crisp, black uniforms and a menu of exotic-sounding coffee concoctions, the café had taken the concept, and the price, of coffee drinking to new heights. Although India Coffee House continued to have its own loyal clientele, Barista had become the hotspot for the young, happening crowd of Lucknow.

As Rahul entered, pushing open the glass door, he saw Feroze already sitting at a corner table, waiting for him. Feroze was wearing a black half jacket, called *sadri* in Lucknow, over a crisp, white kurta and jeans. The casual, carefree look suited Feroze, thought Rahul, as he settled in opposite him. He himself was dressed more conventionally, in a shirt, baggy trousers and black leather shoes.

'Hi, Dinesh couldn't make it this time either.' Rahul said. 'I had called up his home but Amrita said he had gone out.'

There was a third empty chair at the small circular table where the two friends sat. Rahul assumed Feroze had kept the chair in anticipation of Dinesh. Feroze went over to the counter and ordered an espresso for himself and a cappuccino for Rahul. It was Barista that had made them realize that espresso was a dark, thick variety of coffee and not the steam-frothed, milky coffee they were used to having at wedding parties. Feroze remembered how, barely a couple of weeks back, he had come here with Ms Basu—to the latter's insistence and his reluctant elation. He had asked for coffee, only to be patiently explained by Ms Basu that the place served a dozen different coffee concoctions. She had also told him how it was no big deal if he didn't know the difference between them. It was quite natural, she had said, and the same as when an Italian or an American didn't understand the difference between, say, rosogolla, barfi and gulab jamun in India.

Ms Basu would be joining Feroze that Sunday. Happy as he was to be meeting Rahul that day, part of him was excited at the prospect of meeting Ms Basu too. He had not told Rahul that she would be joining them, so he wouldn't get embarrassed in case she didn't turn up. So Rahul was pleasantly surprised when a slim, sophisticated young woman, a few years older than them perhaps, walked up to the empty chair and took the seat, almost as a matter of right, and offered him her hand.

'You must be Rahul. I am Ms Basu, Feroze's professor from university. I have heard a lot about you and Dinesh, and now we've finally had the chance to meet.'

Rahul could barely nod and offer a weak, awkward smile to this lady, the like of whom he had never met before. Feroze had never told him anything about Ms Basu and Rahul had not been expecting company. He wished Feroze had warned him beforehand.

Ms Basu left a tongue-tied Rahul at the table, walked up to the counter where Feroze stood and added her cold coffee without ice cream to the order. She made a futile but sincere attempt to pay, but Feroze would have none of it.

By the time Feroze and Ms Basu rejoined Rahul, the latter had managed to recover from his stunned silence and found himself quite interested in the conversation, which was largely steered by Ms Basu. Although she was not an especially talkative person, the company and comfort of Feroze induced her to speak about things and ideas that needed an outlet in her solitary life. Though she did not quite realize it herself, she liked the company of Feroze, who was so different from her in his upbringing, culture, religion and family but who still shared a silent resonance of ideas and values with her. Soon, Rahul, too, started contributing to the conversation, and words started flowing in a way they wouldn't have if only the two friends had met that Sunday morning at Barista.

While keeping up with the conversation, Rahul kept a keen eye on his friend, trying to detect any sign in his behaviour that would throw light on how and since when the two had been going out for coffee. It was obvious that Ms Basu had great affection for Feroze and that Feroze respected her too, but beyond that, Rahul couldn't glean from the conversation. Their words continued to traverse centuries and miles, ideas and history, skimming topics that were both fascinating and remote from the two friends' immediate concerns of livelihood, career and relationships.

Dinesh had never consciously decided to join politics, but neither had he ever written it off. Even when he left his engineering college, he had no clear idea about what he wanted to do with his life. Of one thing he was sure, though—he didn't want a regular nine-to-five job, whether government or corporate. But he realised, as soon as he landed in Lucknow that day when his father had had that accident, that the situation would never be the same again.

He realized, for the first time, what his father meant to so many people—not only to those of his native village in the district of Allahabad, where they had huge tracts of ancestral farmland, guava orchards, an old, rambling mansion and families dependent on him for everything big and small, but also to those from Raja Saheb's constituency, which was situated in the mango belt in the Lucknow district, in the heart of Awadh, hardly a few miles from the state capital.

On the very first weekend after his return, as Dinesh was sitting in the covered verandah of their government bungalow—

which was still allotted in the name of Raja Saheb, although he was no longer a minister—he was told by Ramdeen that a villager had come to see him. Although it was a common enough event, especially on weekends, of people seeking an audience with his father, it was the first time that someone outside his immediate circle of friends and family had come to see Dinesh.

The villager's name was Dhyanchand and he had come all the way from distant Purab Sharira, hoping to find Raja Saheb or his son. Dinesh had no clue how a poor villager from such a remote village could even know Dinesh had come back. He wondered if the poor, wizened man, with his sun-scorched, leathery skin and rough, white stubble, sitting on his haunches opposite him, had just taken a chance. Or was he just making up a story to appeal to Dinesh's ego?

'Saheb, the people of the tehsil have taken away my tractor. How can I plough my field without it? Please do something, anything, or I will be ruined. The field will turn fallow. How will we survive then? On what will we live?' Dinesh could barely understand the rural dialect Dhyanchand was using, as the words rushed out in a torrent of anxiety.

Dinesh was at a loss. He could guess, from the little experience he had gathered from his childhood visits to their native village on summer vacations, that the farmer must have owed money to a government agency and that the tehsil officials had confiscated his tractor in lieu of the dues as a coercive way to make him pay.

'Why? Do you owe money to the tehsil? Have you paid your land dues?' Dinesh asked to confirm his suspicions.

'Not to the tehsil but to the bank. The bank manager had

promised me he wouldn't send the RC to the tehsil, but I didn't know that he got transferred. Without the tractor how will I plough my land? The tractor will rust in the rains, and if I do get it back later, there will be nothing left in it. They may even auction it. The amin was telling me that the new tehsildar is very strict and will not listen to anybody or anything.'

Dhyanchand was close to tears and Dinesh was by now convinced he was not making things up. The harrowing anxiety, the despondence about the fallow fields, a father's angst at the thought of his hungry children and the silent, invisible fatality of a destroyed future were all writ large on his face.

'How much do you owe the bank?' Dinesh asked.

'I don't know, Saheb. Nobody told me—neither the block people, nor the amin, nor the people of the bank. But what is the point of trying to find out, Saheb? Whatever the amount may be, I have nothing. Will you call up SDM Saheb and ask him to release the tractor, at least till my fields are ploughed, at least till that time?' Dhyanchand pleaded.

Dinesh now finally knew what the man expected of him. He was somewhat relieved to know that the poor farmer didn't expect Dinesh to pay his dues for him, as he didn't have the sort of money the bank would need. He wanted to find out why and how Dhyanchand had taken the loan in the first place, when he didn't have the means to pay it back, when he didn't know how long repayment would take or how the interest would keep piling up against his name in the inscrutable ledgers of the bank. Dinesh, however, knew he had to do something, whether or not it eventually helped Dhyanchand.

Dhyanchand had no idea about the SDM's phone number.

He obviously believed that Dinesh would know, as his father had done. 'In the long run, everybody will be dead, and it is the time till then that matters,' Dinesh remembered reading somewhere.

A couple of calls to the DM's 'camp office' got him the SDM's Malihabad residence phone number. The officer, contrary to the government's explicit orders, continued to live in the city, only making a show of maintaining the government-owned SDM bungalow at Malihabad by keeping a few 'home guards' posted there.

Dinesh had to introduce himself as the son of Raja Surendra Singh, the erstwhile deputy chief minister of the state and still the sitting MLA of Malihabad, first to the orderly who picked up the phone and then to the SDM himself. It was the first time he was directly talking to an officer on someone else's behalf, and he had the lurking suspicion that it was not going to be his last. The SDM was politely adamant, clearly enjoying his power over Dinesh.

'I understand, but something has to be paid before the tractor can be released. I can see to it that his dues are broken down into instalments—and that, too, because you are calling up.' The arguments and bargaining went on for a few more minutes before it was settled that at least ₹10,000, much lower than the initial figure the SDM had suggested, had to be deposited with the tehsil to get the tractor released. As Dinesh replaced the receiver on the cradle, he wondered whether he could have persisted and got a better deal, but the conversation had already left him exasperated.

It was soon clear to Dinesh that Dhyanchand did not even have ₹1,000, but the man didn't seem hopeless. If he expected

Dinesh to pay up for him, he never mentioned it. Perhaps there was an unwritten code of obligation and favour between the elected and the elector that Dinesh's father had carefully crafted over the years that Dinesh was yet to figure out. But Dinesh was mighty glad to see the back of the poor man, covered by a coarse, dusty kurta, as the farmer trudged back out of the large black gates of the bungalow to the traffic junction with the malfunctioning lights that nobody cared about. As the distance between them increased, Dinesh's mind was brought back to his own life and the day that stretched before him. He decided to meet his friends Feroze and Rahul. It had been a long time—much too long, he realized.

Feroze's father was an old man. As far as he could remember, Janaab Zaheer Zaidi, or Zaidi Saheb, had always had grey stubble and hair. Feroze's father, and before him Feroze's grandfather, had been the 'naib' for the Raja of Rasoolabad—a kind of a revenue accountant and chief assistant rolled into one for his vast estates. The estate, adjoining the district of Lucknow, had been with the family for generations, from even before the British came to India. Although Rasoolabad was an ancient hereditary zamindari, it was not a 'princely state', but the family maintained all outward pretensions of being one, including keeping the title of Raja, a king. Indian independence, some 50 years ago, had led to an almost final and fatal turn of events in the fortunes of the family, as had been the case with many taluqedar families of Awadh. First, the Zamindari Abolition

Act, promulgated in the initial days of socialistic idealism, had forced the family to surrender vast tracts of its hereditary estate for a measly compensation. Secondly, their urban properties, worth crores and situated in the very heart of Lucknow, had been declared 'enemy property' in the aftermath of the Indo-Pak War of 1965, as the father of the present raja had emigrated to Pakistan soon after independence and partition. Even then, the fortunes of the family, and its pretensions, had persisted, and Feroze's father's services were still needed and valued. But Zaidi Saheb had realized long ago that his son's life could no longer be tied to the rapidly and irreversibly dwindling fortunes of the Rasoolabad family and that Feroze needed to chart his own course.

Although Feroze respected many of the virtues of his father, and although Zaidi Saheb secretly prided himself on how Feroze had shouldered his family's responsibility at such a young age, their relationship was marked with distances and silences.

'How are your studies going? I hope you are being able to take time out from the job at the newspaper office.' It was a holiday and both father and son were at home.

'Yes, Abbu.' Feroze wanted to add something to his reply but couldn't figure out what. They were sitting in the courtyard, around which stood the rooms of the ancient mansion that had been with the family for so many generations.

'You know I was not in favour of your joining a job so early in life.' It was the umpteenth time that Zaidi Saheb had voiced his reservations for everybody in the family to hear and perhaps to appreciate as well. It was wholly unnecessary. Nobody, least of all Feroze, blamed his father for Feroze's taking up work so early in his life to support his parents and two unmarried sisters. The guilt, however, persisted in the depths of Zaidi Saheb's conscience and showed itself that morning. Feroze didn't know what to say. It was one such day when thoughts hung large in the air but only small nothings could be uttered.

'How is your job going?' Zaidi Saheb asked again.

Feroze didn't want his vocation as a journalist to be reduced to a mere job but knew his father would perhaps not understand. He did, however, know that since he had joined the *Times of Hindustan*, *Inquilaab* had been replaced at home with the English daily, despite Urdu being Zaidi Saheb's language of choice. The fact that Feroze's mother and sisters could hardly read English didn't matter much.

'It is going fine. I am learning and my editor appreciates my work.' Feroze was being truthful and this time managed to prolong his reply, so as not to appear abrupt. Though he had answered truthfully, he knew that his work environment could not be understood through the simple prism of values that dominated Zaidi Saheb's life.

Since his childhood, Feroze had seen his Abbu going about his duties to the family of Rasoolabad with the utmost dedication and loyalty, tinged almost with piety. He had also observed how the old Rasoolabad zamindar, Akhtar Hussain Saheb, treated his Abbu with respect. It was a relationship that went much beyond what could be expected between employer and employee in the current world guided solely by commerce and economics.

To Feroze, his father, this old, rambling mansion, the zamindars of Rasoolabad and even his old editor at *Inquilaab*, Hisam Saheb, represented another age, another system of values where open talk of monetary and commercial transactions were eschewed in polite conversation.

Feroze thought that even Mr Ghosh belonged, in large part, to that old world. It was increasingly apparent to Feroze how commercial interests, even in a reputed newspaper such as his, were increasingly interfering with domains that had hitherto been the sole preserve of the editorial team. Especially since the new managing director had taken over the 'business', the bottom line had started becoming more important than the headline. Feroze knew that Mr Ghosh was perhaps the last bastion of editorial integrity that stood in the way of a complete takeover by the management. He feared what would follow once Mr Ghosh left, whenever that was.

Mr Ghosh was in an exceptionally pensive mood that morning. Even at his best, the editor was never a gregarious and extroverted person. He was calm, clear-sighted and let the young reporters such as Feroze learn on the job while gently guiding them where necessary. But today Mr Ghosh didn't appear to Feroze to be in his usual frame of mind. Mangeram had conveyed to Feroze as soon as he had entered office that Mr Ghosh wanted to see him. Feroze had no clue why and was still waiting to find out.

'Feroze, I will come straight to the point. You know that I have never interfered with your reports, apart from gentle corrections and paraphrasing, and have even given you as much space and placement in the paper as you have desired.' Feroze felt that Mr Ghosh was avoiding looking straight at him.

'I know, sir. You have been supportive and fair.' Feroze replied, as he felt he had to say something.

'I have been, over the past couple of months, getting calls from the MD's office about how critical our editorial content has been appearing to the government.' Mr Ghosh continued. 'Of course, there was no reason for me to share such communication with my staff.'

As a young reporter, this was virgin territory for Feroze, and although he had felt a growing coldness between Mr Ghosh and the marketing head and the general manager of the office, and had even overheard the latter complaining about dwindling advertisements and response from the state government, he had never imagined that the MD himself, the virtual owner of the vast newspaper empire, would be bothered about what he, or anybody else in Lucknow, was writing. He could hardly imagine how Mr Ghosh must have responded to those phone calls, how he would have defended his boys and his own judgement. He wondered what had happened that had prompted Mr Ghosh to single him out that morning.

It was as if to answer Feroze's silent query that Mr Ghosh pulled out a sheaf of papers from his desk drawer. It was not difficult for Feroze to recognize, even from a distance, the story that he had typed out and filed a couple of days ago about the calamitous pollution in the Gomti River. Till then, he had been wondering why his story had not been carried; he had even imagined that it was due to a lack of space because of advertisements, and that the desk had withheld his story to do it full justice when it did appear. Apparently, he was wrong. But Feroze was sure he was not wrong about the contents and the facts of the story. He had checked all the data from the Pollution Control Board and had a copy of the latest test results as well. Feroze was surprised that this story would be considered critical of the government. The newspaper routinely carried reports about the state of affairs in different areas—education, health, law and order—and usually showed how, in all such spheres, things were far from ideal.

'Sir, I really don't find anything objectionable in this story from the government's point of view. Even if there was, I am sure it is not our business to hide the truth, even if it does appear critical of the government. Pollution of the principal river of the state capital concerns public welfare and should be a matter of public knowledge.' Feroze realized, as soon as he had spoken, that he had pre-empted Mr Ghosh. His editor had not yet pointed out why the story was objectionable or what he intended to do with it.

'Feroze, as an editor and as a senior in your profession, I can tell you that it is a solid story and fulfils all the criteria of good journalism, if that is any consolation to you.' Mr Ghosh appeared to be a bit more calm and collected.

'You would know, as I do too, that the greatest contribution to the pollution of the Gomti today is Lucknow Distilleries, situated on its banks. But what you perhaps do not know, as I certainly didn't, is that this old, British-time distillery has recently been taken over by Sheshmani Pandey, nephew and heir apparent to Vibhuti Narayan Pandey, Chief Minister of the state.'

So that was it! It was immediately clear to Feroze how this particular story could damage the Chief Minister's reputation and be used by the opposition to put pressure on the closure of the distillery, thus putting Sheshmani Pandey, and by extension his uncle, under tremendous political and financial pressure. But Feroze was still perplexed about how the MD's office in Bombay had come to know of the proposed story and appreciate its potential fallout. If Mr Ghosh had not known about the recently acquired ownership of Lucknow Distilleries, there was no question of him having alerted the MD's office. Further, Feroze knew that it was not in the nature of Mr Ghosh to show editorial content to the MD beforehand. At the most, he would consult, in general terms, with the executive editor sitting in Bombay, the head of editorial content of the vast newspaper empire. Or that is what Feroze had assumed so far.

'Feroze, this piece will not appear in the newspaper. It does not give me any pleasure to tell you this and in a way it compromises my own judgement and position, but I can tell you that life goes on and that one battle does not necessarily define it. I wanted to tell you this myself, so you would know the whole picture. I know you would have asked questions anyway if your story hadn't appeared in print.' Mr Ghosh had announced the verdict.

Feroze knew he couldn't argue with his editor about the purpose, merit or the accuracy of the story. After all, it was only a few minutes ago that Mr Ghosh had admitted as such. There was nothing more left in the conversation; one could not preach to a convert. The newspaper would continue to print the next day. And the Gomti would continue to flow polluted.

After the completion of their engineering course, both Dinesh and Geeta had moved back to Lucknow. Dinesh was aware that Geeta lived in a government bungalow with a red and green gate and that it was allotted to her father as senior chief engineer in the Public Works Department. He was also aware that the bungalow was indeed closer to his own house than Gita's hostel had been to his. But where physical distance had shrunk, their meetings had become rare and stilted. While in their fourth year they had spent a lot of time together, to Dinesh's disappointment, here in his own hometown, their meetings had become few and far between—and on the rare occasion that they did meet, the interactions were short and wholly unsatisfactory, at least to Dinesh.

Lucknow was still a provincial town of North India, where the meeting of a boy and a girl unrelated by familial ties was uncommon. Though Dinesh could see that since he had left for college, things had changed and college kids would now go out as couples to the newly opened café at Hazratganj, Dinesh found it difficult, nay almost impossible, to ask Geeta out for a cup of coffee. If Geeta's behaviour in college was any indication, she would probably have liked to spend time with Dinesh, but some unarticulated fear and hesitation stopped him every time he thought of asking her. It was fear that Geeta would not reciprocate his own eagerness and that he would lose whatever rare opportunity he still had to enjoy her company.

In fact, the couple of times they had met since their return from Pune had been through Amrita. Quite unknown to Dinesh, Amrita had joined a local NGO that worked for the uplift and empowerment of women artisans in Lucknow.

These women spent their entire lives doing chikankari work, a back-breaking hand embroidery style that paid the artisans a measly amount for the gruelling hours they put in. Dinesh remembered how amazed he was the first time that Amrita had explained her passionate involvement in her work. Dinesh was surprised at how much his sister had grown up in the years they had lived away from each other. It was in the office of this NGO that Amrita had met Geeta quite by accident. Dinesh often wondered, but was again fearful of imagining, if destiny were indeed throwing him a chance, giving him some hope to hold on to.

Dinesh didn't know but would have greatly loved to find out how Amrita and Geeta had met, how they had conversed and bonded, and how one day they had discovered that they both had Dinesh in common. Dinesh couldn't permit himself to think that Geeta would've remembered him as anything more than a good friend.

He remembered the first time the three of them had gone out together. Amrita and Geeta were getting ready to go to Hazratganj for chaat when Dinesh had come home. Amrita had told Dinesh earlier about Geeta, so he was not completely taken aback at finding his old batchmate in their drawing room. It was Geeta who had asked Dinesh to join them.

'Hi, why don't you also come along? We were planning to go Ganjing, maybe have some chaat at Shuklaji's or some coffee at Rovers.' Geeta had asked in her usual spontaneous way, looking straight at him. Dinesh was both elated and hesitant. He didn't want to accept, even to himself, how happy he felt at seeing Geeta in their drawing room that day.

'Yes, we can go. I wonder if you two have gone to the new café that has opened in Hazratganj, where the old Ranjana restaurant used to be. Feroze and Rahul were saying that it is a nice place and is pretty popular with the young crowd,' Dinesh had replied.

'Yes, we can go there too. I have been there. It is quite nice and modern.' Geeta had stood up, ready to go. Amrita did the same. Despite himself, Dinesh had found himself curious about when and with whom Geeta had visited the café, but then realized how little he knew of Geeta's life in Lucknow, her friends, her family, the circles she moved in and the work she did. It was different from their engineering days. Their lives, although moving close to each other in the same city, were still operating on different planes. Breaking his train of thought, Amrita had led them both to their old jalopy, Dinesh had taken the steering wheel, smiling at the pleasant turn the evening had taken.

Dinesh had never been keen to join politics. He had seen how the mad rush of politics had not only taken his father away from family life but also led his mother to live a life of loneliness and suffocation. He remembered how his and Amrita's life had changed, living among complete strangers. He had seen his father change from the idealistic, Left-leaning youth leader to a politician who would rationalize petty compromises in the name of political expediency, and how cut-throat political competition had started to dim his original purpose of serving people and society.

And yet Dinesh found himself unable to escape the multifarious expectations people of his father's constituency and those of their ancestral estate, had of him. He almost felt obliged to fulfil them, as if by remaining aloof he was betraying his father and his legacy. While one day it would be intervention as an extra-legal arbitrator in a family dispute over land, on another it would be a request to call up the local police officer to see that some poverty-stricken prisoner in custody was not treated inhumanly, and on others it would be to just get a hand pump installed in a village. By word of mouth, news spread that Dinesh was ready and willing to help the people, and the number of villagers who came to see him increased by the day.

Often he felt overwhelmed, sometimes irritated, at the seemingly irrational expectations people had, especially those who were well off and felt entitled to ask Dinesh for a favour. There were requests to ring up the principal of the local convent school for some ward's admission or for a room at the Uttar Pradesh Bhawan in Delhi. He often came across the barrier of authority while intervening in matters and sometimes felt that he had no official standing to do so. After all, he was not an MLA or a minister, and he had come to recognize the barely concealed irritation in the voices of some officers when he introduced himself as the son of Raja Surendra Singh, MLA and former Deputy Chief Minister.

So it was with both a feeling of apprehension and relief that Dinesh received Pandeyji's invitation to formally join the party and attend the next executive meeting that was to take place in a fortnight. It was difficult for Dinesh to refuse the old man, a friend of his father's. Vibhuti Narayan Pandey had especially come to Dinesh's house that day, with a fleet of white cars with flashing beacons in tow and a posse of security guards dressed in sharp, steel-grey uniforms. Dinesh was not sure whether Pandeyji had come to enquire after his old friend or to ask Dinesh himself to join the party. He must have known that Dinesh would not be able to refuse him face to face.

That was one of the rare days when Raja Surendra Singh had regained consciousness and was aware of his surroundings. He could hear and understand the voices around him, although he himself couldn't speak. Those were the days that Dinesh tried to spend as much time as he could with his father. Pandeyji, in his own usual halting, soft manner of speaking, explained to his bedridden friend and once-rival how he wanted Dinesh to join the party and how he felt that, with his qualities of heart and mind, his son would one day be a worthy successor to his political legacy. Dinesh didn't particularly like the political legacy bit—if at all he did decide to join politics, it would be his choice, his own course of action—but he didn't disrupt the one-sided conversation between the two men. He knew that only time would tell what the course of his life would be.

'You know how we have been looking for young people to join politics. After all, we are growing old. I feel the age now in my bones and yet the next generation is not ready to understand and shoulder the responsibilities. When I look at Dinesh, I see a ray of hope.' Pandeyji was speaking to his friend. The last rays of the sun were filtering in through the gaps in the curtain. Amrita had come in a few minutes earlier to serve Pandeyji a cup of tea, had touched his feet and received a profusion of blessings. Dinesh once again realized how different the two siblings had become—Dinesh could never imagine touching anyone's feet, not even his father's.

'I see in Dinesh a young Raja Surendra Singh, the one who had joined politics years ago, a young, idealistic man who had his heart and mind in the right place. Dinesh will attend the coming state executive meeting of the party, and by that time I will take the party high command into confidence and announce a formal position for him. It will help him get official recognition in the party and give him a start in his career.'

The Chief Minister had already assumed that Dinesh would say yes—he was only sharing his plans with his silent friend. Although the old, bedridden man was unable to speak, that evening he looked at Dinesh and then back at the Chief Minister. To Dinesh, it appeared that his father agreed with the course of action his old friend and superior had chalked up for his son.

The sun had set and the room was getting dark. As Dinesh switched on the tubelight, he realized that he would have to make a decision soon, or people and events would overtake him. He suddenly felt as if he were being swept along by the mighty current of a wild river, a river far from the gentle, lazy Gomti he had grown up seeing.

Even as Rahul spent most of his time preparing for the civil service exams, or the UPSC, he tried to do justice to his post-graduate engineering course. It helped that he had decided on engineering as one of his chosen subjects for the civil service exams, but even more than that, he felt obliged to make an effort due to the scholarship money the government was providing for his post-graduation.

The other subject that Rahul had chosen was History. Rahul remembered how Feroze had introduced him to Ms Basu that Sunday morning. He admitted that he owed much of his recently acquired interest in history to the stimulating conversations he had shared with both of them since. Ms Basu had not only recommended books to Rahul but had also lent him many without any self-conscious generosity. However, Rahul realized that for all his intellectual curiosity, for him history was just a means to clear the civil service exams—and he always read the books with an eye on the syllabus. But for Ms Basu, and increasingly for Feroze, history was something else. They read from primary sources, from multiple authors on the same subject for their varying interpretations, and applied their own minds to it. Ms Basu showed them how to resurrect history from the depths of time, looking for and linking clues that lay across time and space to arrive at insights.

Although Rahul enjoyed the conversations the three of them had, he sometimes felt guilty for infringing on Feroze's and Ms Basu's time. Today, however, was special, as along with the three of them, Dinesh and his one-time college mate, Geeta, would be joining them for evening tea. Rahul had met Geeta once before, when he had accidentally come across Dinesh, Amrita and Geeta at Hazratganj. All three of them were blissfully enjoying golgappas from a streetside vendor. Dinesh had introduced Geeta to his childhood friend then, and Rahul remembered noticing how shy, awkward and smitten Dinesh had been in her presence.

Rahul was the last to arrive at the tea bar, a newly opened joint in Gomti Nagar, and all five pairs of eyes—Amrita was also there—looked up at him. They appeared to be in the middle of banter, and laughter shone in their eyes. The rays of the afternoon sun, filtering through overladen monsoon clouds, flooded the interiors. It was Dinesh who had insisted on meeting here, as Geeta was more of a tea than a coffee person. Rahul had also noticed the old, white Chevrolet parked outside the tea bar and remembered the days when the three of them would drive to Rovers or Moti Mahal in it after a Sunday cricket match.

There were a surprising number of tea varieties on the menu, some he had never heard of before. For him, tea was the standard Red Label Brooke Bond his mother made with milk and sugar and served him every morning with Parle-G or Marie biscuits. It was left to Ms Basu to order for all of them, though she did ask everyone. It was only Geeta, Rahul observed, who carefully went through the menu and decided to 'experiment' with something called 'Makaibari'. Apparently, the name came from the exotic tea garden high up in the Darjeeling hills where the tea was sourced from.

Rahul, Dinesh, Feroze and Amrita had all opted for 'Kulhad Ki Chai', tea served in earthen tumblers, a common sight on railway stations all over India. This humble variety, which had now become somewhat of an 'in' thing among the young, ironically had its origins in India's centuries-old caste prejudices. Ms Basu ordered a classic Assam tea for herself.

Once the waiter had left after taking their orders, the conversation started to relax, as no one was in any particular hurry. Though there were varying degrees of familiarity between them, and though Geeta was meeting Ms Basu for the first time, there was no barrier of awkwardness between them.

'How are your preparations going for the civils?' Ms Basu asked Rahul, referring to the preliminary examination of the UPSC, to be held in a fortnight.

'It is ok. Of course, there is a lot of luck and uncertainty involved, and I am appearing for the first time,' Rahul replied.

'I am sure you are going to clear it. You were always the topper type,' Dinesh said, with genuine belief and pride. But Rahul knew that thousands of such 'topper types' appeared in the examinations every year, many of them armed with years of preparation and even those with failed previous attempts. He had heard that there were entire localities in Delhi, Patna, Lucknow and other large cities across north India where students lived in rented apartments and hostels for years together, just preparing for the exams as an annual ritual.

'I know you opted for engineering for the prelims, but if you require any help in history for the mains, feel free to let me know.' Rahul knew Ms Basu's concern was genuine.

'I know, Ma'am.' Rahul, like Feroze, addressed Ms Basu as Ma'am, although she was hardly five years older than them and had, long ago, graduated from her role as a mere teacher to something closer to a friend, philosopher and guide.

'Give her a break. We can call her by her name, can't we?' Geeta addressed herself to Ms Basu directly, although she was meeting her for the first time.

'Yes, of course. I would be glad if all of you called me by my first name—Sharmila—though it does not quite fit with my personality.' Ms Basu laughed out loud. 'Sharmila' in Hindi meant 'shy', a name that perhaps suited Amrita more, who had not spoken a single word till then. However, from the look on her face, she was clearly enjoying the company and the conversation.

'I have finally decided to join politics full time.' Dinesh announced to the gathering.

They knew that Dinesh had joined his father's party and had even been appointed to the state executive some time back, but he had still been undecided about his intentions to join politics full time, at least till then.

'And what made you finally take the plunge?' Feroze asked.

Dinesh uttered something light-heartedly about politics being the last resort of the scoundrel, but inside he knew that by the time he had decided to take the plunge, he was already in deep waters and there was no way out.

It appeared to Rahul that both Amrita and Geeta had prior knowledge of Dinesh's decision and that this was news only to Feroze and himself.

It was also at that moment that Feroze realized that his childhood friend had now become a news item, and that his conversations with Dinesh could take on a different hue. He remembered Mr Ghosh telling him once that pure friendship between a politician and a journalist was difficult to sustain. Another thought, too, struck him: if Rahul did succeed in clearing the civil service examinations and went on to become an IAS officer, would Feroze's relationship with him change too? Despite such thoughts, Feroze inwardly wished his friends the best in their careers and hoped their friendship would withstand the differences life may throw at them. He wondered whether his friends, too, felt the same way.

Never had Feroze seen his father, Zaidi Saheb, in such a frame of mind. It was as if the very foundation of his belief system had given way and he didn't know how to make sense of the abyss. Even in the days when their locality in old Lucknow had been threatened with communal disturbances, Feroze remembered his father to be full of faith, hope and action, and had even seen him volunteering as a civil defence warden. But this time it was different.

Feroze knew the reason behind his father's disconsolate frame of mind. It was in his own newspaper a few days back. The Government of India had decided to introduce a Bill in Parliament to amend the existing Enemy Property Act. The immediate effect of the changed law was that the government would be able to declare the extensive urban properties of the Raja of Rasoolabad as enemy property, thus bypassing the recent Supreme Court judgement in the raja's favour.

Feroze knew it had been a long-standing dispute. The estates of the Raja of Rasoolabad were first declared enemy property in the aftermath of the 1965 Indo-Pak War, on the grounds that the grandfather of the present Raja had emigrated to Pakistan just after Partition. But his sons and grandsons had all stayed back in India, and the present Raja, in his youth, had even represented the city in the Indian Parliament. Naturally, the family had taken the matter to court, and after decades of legal hearings, the Supreme Court had declared a few months back that the order of the government to declare the estates enemy property was illegal. For the Raja of Rasoolabad, and by extension Zaidi Saheb, the judgement had been a vindication of their faith in the country's justice system and a reinforcing of their place under the Indian sun. The effect of the new Bill, however, was an unravelling of all that.

Feroze had been following the opposing opinions on the subject, both in the streets of Lucknow and in the pages of local newspapers. Those occupying the properties of the Raja of Rasoolabad, who had been given to believe in their rights by generations of politicians, were against the court judgement, their fear of eviction fuelled by the uncertainty around their collective futures. Many of them belonged to families that had fled their homes in West Punjab in 1947 and relocated in the city, rebuilding their future through decades of struggle and austerity. The prospect of all that vanishing into thin air one fine morning was too much for them to even contemplate.

Feroze was aware that these families were putting enormous pressure on the ruling party, and that they were collectively crucial to it as a vote bank. The young national president of the ruling party was now a Member of Parliament from Lucknow, and all these families—with their branches and extensions—were vital votes for his re-election.

Feroze was still new to the newspaper but felt Mr Ghosh had started to rely on him for some of the more important assignments, even when senior reporters were available. Some of them, such as Mr Swami and Mr Shah, didn't seem to mind and even encouraged Feroze, but Monica, five years his senior, was different. Monica had been covering the Chief Minister's beat and that of the ruling party for years, even when she was a staff reporter in another publication. She had developed extensive connections and acquaintances, which enabled her to break exclusive stories frequently. But Feroze felt that none of those stories were ever critical of the Chief Minister or the Prime Minister. Even when her stories appeared to be against the government, they were directed at a rival minister or power centre that needed to be put in place. Perhaps, Feroze thought, that was the price you paid to maintain those connections.

Mr Ghosh had once again singled out Feroze to do an exclusive interview, this time of the Raja of Rasoolabad. Although reams of newsprint had been devoted to the issue, the raja himself had remained elusive, refusing any interview on the matter. Perhaps Mr Ghosh had thought that Feroze's father's connection with the Rasoolabad family would let Feroze in. And he was right: the only condition the old raja put forward to Feroze was that he travel to the Rasoolabad Fort, a few miles into the countryside, to meet him, as his health did not permit him to travel by road.

So it was that after travelling some 70 odd miles, Feroze found himself sitting opposite the old man one evening in his old, rambling mansion. Feroze had met the raja many times as a child when he had accompanied his father on Eid and other special occasions, but the man now appeared to be much more frail than he remembered.

'Do you feel wronged by the government, especially since you were once a Member of Parliament from the ruling party yourself?' It was the first incisive question after the warm-ups, during which Feroze's photographer and friend Peter had managed to take a few shots of the raja in the fading sunlight that peeped through the enormous French windows of the palatial room.

'Yes, as a matter of fact, I do. I believe that if my friend and colleague, the late prime minister, had been alive and Raja Surendra Singh had not been incapacitated by that terrible accident, the government would not have decided to press for a new law to declare our estates enemy property.' The raja was never one to mince words. Perhaps, as Feroze had heard, that had been the reason why he had never returned to electoral politics after his maiden stint in Parliament.

'Sir, don't you think, as many people have suggested, that in today's day and age, such huge hereditary and feudal properties cannot be justified, especially in a poor country as ours?' Feroze had heard this popular assertion many a time in the streets and the shops of Hazratganj, where a large number of the raja's properties lay.

'Look, if our properties had been taken under an urban-property-ceiling law, I would have understood, but to declare us enemies of the nation after all these years is intolerable.' The raja was now visibly agitated. 'My father and I have lived in this land our whole lives. I have been a Member of Parliament. We have always been proud Indians—and now, just because my grandfather migrated to Pakistan decades ago, to say that we were and are enemies of the country is preposterous! If that is the case, where do we belong? I want an answer from the Prime Minister himself.'

The interview, Feroze realized, was turning out to be sensational and if he could do any justice to it, the story was national first-page material. Tea had been served in heavy silverware, as had always been the tradition in the Rasoolabad household. As the chandelier was switched on, the memory of another such interview struck Feroze—the one he had taken of

Raja Surendra Singh a couple of years back, which had given him his very first journalistic break.

He hoped this would be his next.

Rahul woke up with a start. The bus had come to a sudden halt in front of the towering gates of the Lal Bahadur Shastri National Academy of Administration, or the Mussoorie Academy, as it was popularly called. A few of them from Lucknow had managed to hire the minibus that had started the previous evening from Charbagh and had taken them—the young, starry-eyed qualifiers of the civil service exams—to the academy. It was still dark outside and the moon appeared to be hanging over the shoulder of a distant hill, as if still undecided about whether to bid adieu to the night. There was a slight chill in the air and some of the young men and women were pulling out their sweaters and pullovers from their bags. Rahul's own woollens were packed in the suitcases that lay tied up, hopefully securely, on the roof of the bus. Fortunately, the guards standing at the gates of the academy had prior knowledge of their arrival and let the bus enter the hallowed portals that was the dream and destination for all of them.

Rahul considered himself extremely lucky to have not only cleared the tough exams but also to have got into the IAS 'proper' on his very first attempt. The others in the minibus—Rahul knew a couple of them from the days he had joined a short course to prepare for the UPSC interview—were joining different civil services: foreign service, the police, forest service, railway service, etc. All of them had been invited to the Mussoorie Academy for a three-month foundation course, after which the IAS officer trainees would stay back and the others would move on to their respective national academies in other parts of the country—Hyderabad, Faridabad, Nagpur, Simla, Delhi and Vadodara.

Those three months, and the six-month professional course afterwards, when the academy would feel quieter and lonelier, would go off in a haze of activity—lectures, horse rides, treks, adventures, sports and exercises, fun and frolic, studies and tests. And yet those days would leave an imprint on their young minds that would only become dearer and deeper as the years went by. But, of course, at that time, neither Rahul nor the other officer trainees knew it.

'I wonder when the state cadres will be allotted.' It was Shivdarshan, the tall, dark guy from Tamil Nadu.

Rahul and a few others were sitting near the open space in front of Ganga Dhaba, technically just outside the academy but very much part of it in their collective consciousness. For the past few days, the topic of cadre allocation for members of the All India Services had drowned out every other topic. There had been countless predictions, permutations and combinations that had been tried, sometimes in secret, to predict the state cadres of officer trainees, and yet nobody could tell for certain if their lives would be spent in Maharashtra or Meghalaya, Kerala or Kashmir. Some were more anxious than the others. Shivdarshan belonged to the more anxious group and was almost fearful of getting a northern cadre, never having stepped out of Tamil Nadu in all of his 30 years.

'I guess it will be announced sometime during our Bharat Darshan.' Amresh's father was in the IAS and, as such, he claimed to know more about the norms and ways of the services. Rahul had observed that quite a few of the officer trainees had their father, and sometimes even their mother, in one of the services; a few of them knew each other from before. Rahul, despite not knowing anyone, had never felt like an outsider, as he knew there were many others like him who were the first in their families to have even dared to appear for the UPSC.

'And then the dynamics among us will start changing and some of us will suddenly be more equal than the rest.' It was Rita, giggling away as she spoke, laughing with her eyes as she looked at Padmini across the table. Rahul didn't understand the full import of what Rita had said and felt a bit foolish, but as far as he was concerned, he hadn't given much thought to cadre allotment and how that would affect his life. All of them would have to go to whatever state they were allotted. Maybe he was missing something. Rahul looked at Rita nonchalantly but inside he knew, although he wouldn't admit it, that he wanted to keep looking at her till it was dark outside, till the full moon rose over the Binog hill and everyone had left for their respective hostel rooms. Nobody had ever cast such a spell over Rahul as Rita Kaur, the daughter of Sardar Tejveer Singh, former Cabinet Secretary to the Government of India and Chief Secretary of Haryana. But Rahul knew he was not the only one she had cast a spell over—many of his male colleagues had openly approached and proposed to her, only to be laughingly rejected, without a second thought or even a second look.

'You are very silent this evening. You are sure of getting

your home state, Uttar Pradesh, isn't it? Although I don't know if that's a good thing.' Rita said looking at Rahul. Rahul feared that she had an inkling that she, and not cadre allotment, was the reason behind Rahul's thoughtful silence that evening. But Rahul was sure that girls such as Rita were used to tongue-tied admiration from boys.

'Even I don't know whether that is good or bad. Who can say what will happen in the next 35 years or so in our careers? States that appear today to be progressive and peaceful may suddenly become retrogressive and narrow-minded. Who can tell what lies in future?' Rahul finally managed to utter.

'Que sera sera, whatever will be will be, the future's not ours to see.' Rita, Padmini and Jay sang out in unison, with Rita's voice in obvious lead. All three of them were from Delhi University and were apparently good friends. Rahul felt they moved in a different orbit from his, which led to their easy confidence, self-assurance, comfort in their own skin and even a sense of entitlement.

Rita's prediction turned out to be true and Rahul was allotted his home cadre of Uttar Pradesh a couple of months after that evening at Ganga Dhaba. But whether Rita had any inkling of her own cadre, Rahul was not sure. With her top rank, Rita should have got her home cadre of Haryana and yet, due to some twist of fate, she, too, was allotted Uttar Pradesh as an 'outsider'. Rahul, like that evening at Ganga Dhaba, didn't know whether that was a good thing or a bad thing, for her or for him.

They were to go on to the same state academy for further training and then work in the same state for the rest of their careers. Whether Rita's cadre allotment mattered to her, it was impossible to tell. Neither her giggles, nor her nonchalant demeanour changed—and nor did her attitude towards Rahul. It was as if Rahul, despite being there in front of her, might as well have been invisible.

The monsoons had been both weak and delayed that year and a drought-like situation had developed in many parts of Uttar Pradesh. With better transportation, communication and democracy in post-independence India, famine and starvation deaths were almost unimaginable but there were nevertheless increasing signs of acute agricultural distress, which had started reaching the power corridors of the capital.

The Chief Minister, as state party president, had decided to constitute an informal four-member committee of party office bearers to go to the hinterland on a fact-finding mission. Dinesh knew it was typical of the politician, who had never depended on the feedback he received through official channels as head of the government. He had once confided to Dinesh that the officials sent their reports based on their perception of what their superiors wanted to hear. But Dinesh couldn't imagine why the Chief Minister had decided to include him in the committee.

Although Dinesh's family had extensive agricultural tracts and mango groves in rural areas of the Allahabad region, it was difficult for Dinesh to claim, with his city-bred upbringing, that he was knowledgeable about agriculture, villagers or farmers. But then, he reasoned, Pandeyji's nephew, Sheshmani, was even more out of touch with the rural scene.

The foreign-educated, ambitious politician nephew evoked a sense of unease in Dinesh that he could not put his finger on. Even the fact that the committee was headed by the veteran Member of Parliament Adesh Singhji seemed to irk Sheshmani, although this old, Gandhian politician was politeness personified with everyone. The fourth member of the committee was young Yogendra, whom Dinesh had never met earlier. However, over the next couple of days he grew to like him almost as much as he grew to dislike Sheshmani. Dinesh couldn't explain why some people evoked such feelings in him, of either like or dislike, but as far back as he could remember, it had always been so. More often than not, his relationship with a person matched his initial feelings for him or her. Dinesh remembered it had been the same for Rahul and Feroze.

The jeep in which they were travelling was speeding over a national highway towards Jhansi. They had been touring the interiors of the vast state for the past few days, meeting villagers, gram pradhans, party cadres and government officials, sleeping mostly in government dak bungalows and only once in the palatial residence of a local party chieftain.

'We could have used two vehicles, instead of all of us sitting cramped in one jeep.' Sheshmani remarked to nobody in particular. The air that rushed in through the open windows of the moving vehicle made his remark a bit inaudible and Dinesh was not sure if Adeshji, sitting in front beside the driver, had heard.

'I could have brought my Pajero along,' Sheshmani added. He was extremely proud of his recently acquired red Pajero. It was the very first of the model to have reached Lucknow and he had spared no occasion reminding everyone of that.

'In our times, we would use all kinds of transport—bullock carts, tongas, boats, cycles and the occasional car; we would even walk through farms, from one village to another. It was slow and hard work but it was great experience. I remember how, as a young man, I had accompanied Vinobaji on his Bhoodan yatras over miles, trudging through villages.' Adeshji frequently lapsed into his memories, where selective amnesia made everything beautiful.

'Times have changed, if you and people of your generation would care to see.' Sheshmani never cared for what others thought and was at his acerbic best that day. Dinesh could see that the old man fell silent after Sheshmani's remark and wondered what he thought of dealing with this new, brash successor to his style of politics.

'Your gleaming Pajero, or for that matter Dineshji's Chevrolet, would probably have made the villagers wary of us. It is also possible that your beloved red beauty would bear some resentful scratches at the hands of village urchins. I know because I am from a village and still live in one, unlike you. It is indeed wise not to bring your fancy, flashy cars on such trips.' Yogendra was never one to be silent, especially when he found someone spouting nonsense. It was perhaps this quality that had endeared him to Dinesh. There was nothing that Sheshmani could say after that and he kept looking out of the window, disdainfully aloof.

Empty, brown and dusty farms stretched all the way to the horizon on both sides of the highway. Only the occasional clump of trees, an electricity transmission tower or a filthy roadside dhaba would break the visual monotony. Sheshmani had made it clear that meals, or even a cup of tea at these dhabas was out of the question. He even carried his own thermos of tea, which he, Dinesh had to admit, was ready to share with the rest of them.

Dinesh had been unusually silent that morning and had not uttered a single word since they had left the circuit house in Kanpur. It had been a lifelong habit of his that whenever he was in the countryside, travelling, he felt absorbed in the country scene—not only in the visual delight of the vast, empty landscapes but also in thoughts of the villagers and farmers, their lives and miseries, their ignorance and deprivations, their hopes and unchanging lifestyle, and how indifferent the people in the cities had grown to their plight. Dinesh, however, still lacked the ability to express his thoughts in words and political discourses. Lately, he had started speaking at party forums and had even made a few public speeches during party programmes. He had learnt that his speeches had been noticed and even appreciated in some quarters and that the old Chief Minister himself had remarked somewhere how Dinesh's brand of inclusive politics was the need of the hour. Dinesh didn't know what future he had in politics but felt it would be worthwhile only if it changed, even if marginally, the collective future of these villagers. He looked at Sheshmani and wondered how their different brand of politics—one of empathy with the have-nots and the other of opportunistic deal making; one of hard work and service, and the other of entitlement and power—would play out in future.

'So are you ready to contest the by-elections from the seat your father has resigned?' It was Yogendra asking Dinesh. Raja

Surendra Singh had recently resigned his seat in the legislative assembly, as he felt he was not doing justice to his role as legislator. Many believed Raja Saheb was trying to pave the way for his son's entry into politics but Dinesh knew his father genuinely believed it was ethically and morally wrong for him to cling to his seat when there seemed to be no chance of his discharging his duties in the near future.

'I don't know. It appears to be dynastic politics in one sense, and yet the villagers of my father's constituency want me, and no one else, to represent them. The Chief Minister has offered me a seat in the council too. I am not yet sure about my readiness to contest an election.' Dinesh was being honest.

'You should contest the by-election. The legislative councils and the Rajya Sabha are for those who are past their active lives in electoral politics, who can't win a seat on their own and have to be adjusted somehow.' Nobody had asked for Sheshmani's opinion but he chose to give it, nonetheless. Dinesh realized that Sheshmani was perhaps taking a resentful dig at Adesh Singhji, who was a member of the Rajya Sabha. It was typical of Sheshmani, but it was difficult to tell if Adeshji had heard him. Even if he had, he said nothing.

The jeep came to a slow halt in front of a temporary welcome arch the local party cadres and politicians of Ghatampur had set up. The short, uneventful journey had come to an end and another day of meeting people, listening to their woes, dealing with sycophantic, self-seeking, small-time politicians and interviewing patwaris and tehsildars beckoned them.

Dinesh, however, felt that their four-member committee was not doing enough to find out the concerns and thoughts of one half of the population that lay hidden behind centuries of social barriers—the voiceless, faceless women of the villages. In times such as this, he wondered what it would have been like to have Geeta, and her alone, accompany him on his tours.

Feroze was never one to show his emotions but that day he was so happy that he felt the need to share his joy with someone. Although he had always been a good student, he could never have imagined that he would top the university in the MA examinations. Rajeev, his colleague from another newspaper who covered the education beat, had rung Feroze up a few minutes back on his recently acquired Motorola mobile.

Feroze remembered how two years back he had gone to the university for his graduation results, thinking it would be his last visit to it, and how afterwards he had gone to meet Ms Basu in her chambers. That summer afternoon now felt like a lifetime away. So much had happened since then—he thought about how he had grown, both professionally and individually and in his relationships. He had grown somewhat distant from his family, and although his friendship with Dinesh and Rahul stood fast, it was Ms Basu who had started occupying more of his time and thoughts.

Feroze realized that it was Ms Basu, more than anyone else, with whom he wanted to share his joy that afternoon. It was to her that he owed most of his academic success. A couple of his classmates had rung him up to congratulate him and so had his editor and boss Mr Ghosh. But Ms Basu had not yet called. He wondered why. Had she heard of Feroze's results but expected him to call?

Almost unconsciously, Feroze cycled up to Ms Basu's house on the university road. Over the past few months, Feroze had become an increasingly frequent visitor to the house but knew that he was not the only one. Over the past few years, Ms Basu had started to teach a few students in her house, those she felt had the potential to do better in their studies and who needed her help, guidance and encouragement. Most of them were ambitious, hardworking but needy students from the mofussil towns of Uttar Pradesh, who had almost always studied under indifferent teachers and reached university through sheer grit and hard work. Unlike other university professors, Ms Basu didn't charge them for these 'extra' classes. Although she herself made light of her selfless service and charity, claiming that she anyway earned more than she needed, Feroze knew that what she was doing was exceptional. It only added to his estimation of this remarkable lady.

Today, however, there was no class in progress: Feroze could tell because there were no cycles outside. Indeed, there was an atmosphere of eerie silence in the house, broken only by the sound of the doorbell that Feroze rang. He was ushered in by the wisp of a maid, Bala, who was as devoted to Ms Basu as one would be to one's own family. In fact, it sometimes appeared to Feroze that Bala was the closest Ms Basu had to a family.

'It is one of those days, Feroze sir. She is in her room and not meeting anyone.' Bala was almost whispering, afraid of disturbing her mistress. Both Feroze and Bala knew that Ms Basu's restriction of not meeting anyone didn't apply to Feroze.

Indeed, Ms Basu sat upright on her unmade bed as Feroze entered the semi-dark room.

Sharmila, as Feroze had started calling her when they were alone, had no make-up on, her hair was undone and she was wearing a thin, cotton nightgown, although it was well past noon. As she adjusted the cushions to make herself more comfortable, Feroze couldn't help notice the shapely outline of her figure through the thin, wispy material. He quickly averted his eyes but the vision refused to leave his mind.

'Congratulations, topper saheb. I am so happy at your results. Indeed, I am doubly proud of you, because I know how difficult it must have been for you to manage both your studies and your journalistic commitments.' Ms Basu was visibly happy at Feroze's success but he couldn't help wonder why she hadn't called him up as soon as she had come to know.

'Who told you?' Feroze asked nonchalantly, increasing the speed of the ceiling fan. The room was getting a bit stuffy but given the state of her dress—or rather undress—he dared not open the windows to let the breeze in.

'The same person who informed you. Rajeev called me up and even took a short interview on your success. Of course, every year somebody tops the MA course in History but it is not every year that a successful journalist does it. I am glad it was only after the interview that my mobile phone got discharged, otherwise my interview would not have appeared in tomorrow's newspapers. I am proud of myself too. It is not every day that my interview appears in the city's newspaper. It will tomorrow, thanks to you.'

Feroze knew Sharmila too well to think her own interview

mattered so much to her; he knew it was his success that thrilled her. The fact that it meant so much to her increased his own joy manifold, much more than the fact that he had topped the university. He realized that for him, Sharmila's joy, thrill and satisfaction, her appreciation and acceptance, were much more important than his own success—that it was she, and she alone, with whom he felt the intrinsic need to share his innermost joys. Ms Sharmila Basu, who was that instant lying on her bed in front of him, resting her head in the crook of her elbow, looked up at him with a twinkle in her eyes and a smile on her lips.

'What are you looking at?' Sharmila was nothing if not direct. Feroze felt embarrassed, awkward and at a loss for words, as if Sharmila had somehow read his innermost feelings and sensed his latent attraction for her.

'Nothing. You had better get up and get ready. It is not good to waste the entire day in bed, even if it is a holiday.' Feroze held out his hand.

'I know. I was feeling a bit under the weather since morning but now it is better.' Sharmila was laughing with her eyes, looking at Feroze, as she took his hand to get up from her supine position.

'Let us go and celebrate with your friends. It is an achievement that deserves celebration. I will throw a small party in your honour.' Sharmila announced, as she headed towards the washroom.

Feroze had no great desire to share this moment of joy with anyone else, but his innate sense of loyalty to his friends stopped him from admitting so. He knew both Dinesh and Rahul would be happy and proud of his achievement. He knew that his father, mother and sisters, too, would be happy. He wondered if anybody had told them yet.

Rahul wondered what might have prompted the Appointment department of the Uttar Pradesh government, responsible for the posting of IAS officers, to send him to the district of Barabanki, of all places. Barabanki was not only a neighbouring district of Lucknow but had, over the years, become developed enough to seem like an extension of the ever-expanding capital itself. But then, Rahul surmised, it must have been a coincidence, as there could be no one he knew who could or would influence the government with regard to his posting.

Rita had been posted in Lucknow and, in her case, Rahul guessed there might have been an influential phone call or two from her father or his friends to somebody important in the government. At least that is what their other three batchmates conjectured, who had got posted to far-flung corners of the state—to Kushinagar, Farrukhabad and Lalitpur.

For their three-month stay at the state academy in Aliganj, Lucknow, Rahul had opted to stay at the hostel itself, rather than in his own home. Of course, the rules of the academy stated that every officer trainee had to stay in the hostel, but everyone knew that the rule was rarely followed, especially for trainees such as Rahul who had their homes in the city. Still, he preferred to stay in the sparsely furnished room at the hostel, as he didn't want to behave differently from his batchmates and enjoy the privileges of being a 'city boy'. The fact that it allowed him to stay close to

Rita was an added incentive, which Rahul would have admitted to himself, had he felt he stood any chance with her.

'Will you stay in Barabanki proper or commute from your home in Lucknow? How far is it anyway?' It was Rita who asked Rahul. She was trying to avoid the direct rays of the afternoon sun with the shade of her dupatta. The three of them—Avinash was also there—were sitting in the back lawns of the academy. It was the last day of the course, which had ended earlier that morning with a valedictory function, where a fat and pompous looking officer, the Chairman of the Board of Revenue, had seemed to pontificate on everything under the sun.

'It is not that close. I will have to find accommodation in Barabanki,' Rahul replied. Their other two batchmates had left for their respective districts a few minutes earlier and Rahul found himself wishing that Avinash, otherwise a good friend, had also left along with them. Rahul suspected that Avinash, too, wanted to spend one more evening with Rita. Rahul couldn't really blame him.

'What about you, Avinash? When are you leaving for your district?' Rita turned her gaze towards Avinash.

'Tomorrow, after breakfast, I guess. It is not that far, as I saw on the map. Besides, I am sure Farrukhabad can survive one more day without me.' Avinash was his usual funny self. The academy mess was nearby and they usually sat here in the green back lawns, getting their cups of hot tea from the mess and occasional snacks that Bishtji, the mess manager, would prepare especially for them. Rahul had shared many an evening here with Rita in the last two months, and although their initial banter had graduated into something deeper and more meaningful, Rahul didn't dare assume it was anything more than that. But Rahul felt his heart sinking at the thought of those beauty-drenched evenings and starry nights coming to an end. From the next day, their lives, thrown into the heat and dust of their districts and work, would become irreversibly different. Rahul didn't want to think about that and yet realized that he, and all the others, had opted for this very life.

'I hope you will at least come over on weekends.' Rita was looking directly at him. Rahul was a bit surprised to find that her face, usually merry and laughing, was sombre. Avinash had left just a couple of minutes back to pack his things, leaving the two of them alone. Rahul tried hard to detect if Rita was mocking him, if there was any hint of laughter in her eyes or in the crook of her lips. But there was none.

'I would love to.' Rahul blurted out. He hadn't thought about it before that moment and yet it seemed to be the only possible response. Suddenly, the evening, the green lawns, the flowers gently swaying in the evening breeze, the dance of the white clouds in the late monsoon sky, all started to appear more beautiful in his eyes, made ethereal by the stronger, more radiant beauty in front of him. It was a beauty so real and yet so ephemeral and fragile that Rahul feared to even touch it, let alone embrace it. It was as if a single breath, a single whisper would melt it away.

'I would love it too.' Rahul hoped, and almost imagined, that Rita had actually said the words. But she hadn't. Rita remained silent, perhaps thinking of something else.

Geeta realized that, of late, Amrita had almost become a proxy for her brother Dinesh. It was not that Geeta didn't like Amrita; in fact, she admired her silent dignity, poise and quiet self-assurance. She would also, occasionally, detect the embers of the same idealism that she sensed burning somewhere deep inside Dinesh. That had been the real reason that she had felt attracted to him in college. She wondered at how far removed from this life their college days seemed. She also wondered whether Dinesh ever thought of those days in Pune. Lately, Dinesh had been extremely busy with his nascent political life, especially since he had decided to contest the seat of the legislative assembly that had fallen vacant after Dinesh's father had resigned. Geeta missed those days in Pune.

It was a bright, young morning. Overnight rains had washed the city clean, and everything, from the leaves of the amaltas tree to the flowers of the frangipani plants that lined Vikramaditya Marg and even the usually dirty pavements, appeared bright and cheerful. Geeta and Amrita were sitting on a tonga with their backs to the driver, as it clattered through the heart of the city towards the old Chowk area. Visions of everyday citylife rolled past them like scenes on a cinema reel. Although the two friends were looking at the same things, Geeta wondered whether they saw the same things too.

'Have you ever thought of joining politics?' Geeta had wanted to ask Amrita this for some time now, especially since Dinesh had taken the plunge.

'No, not really. Two in a family of three are, I think, enough.' Amrita laughed and, looking at Geeta, asked. 'Have you?'

Geeta was taken aback. She had imagined that for her,

with her service-class, professional family background, even the question of joining politics didn't arise. Nobody in her family had ever joined politics: it was considered infra dig, the last resort of the scoundrel.

'Of course not. For us, the question does not even arise. For you though, with your family's political background, it seemed like a natural question.' Geeta replied, although somewhere inside she felt that it had not been such a ridiculous question, after all.

For the past few months, both Amrita and Geeta had been part of an NGO called Samriddhi, which worked with the poor women of the old Chowk area of Lucknow. Geeta had observed that while Amrita worked resolutely, with hope and patience, just like the founder couple of the organization Mona Singh and her reclusive husband, Geeta frequently lost patience and got frustrated with the painfully slow progress they seemed to be making with the lives of the women they worked with. She also grew impatient with the hassles and barriers that the ever-present 'system' imposed on them or anybody wanting to do good. Perhaps, if she had been in Amrita's shoes and belonged to a political family, Geeta would actually have joined politics. Maybe she would not have been satisfied with doing such small-scale, patient, constructive work that Amrita and her mentor Ms Singh took such joy in. Her thoughts had just begun to explore the remote possibility of her ever being part of a political family and how she would feel if she did, when the tonga came to a sudden halt in front of the Chowk police station, after having negotiated the throngs in the Nakkhas area of Lucknow. Amrita paid the ever-cheerful tongawalla, Babban

Mian, and started walking through the lanes—under massive, crumbling gates, past hoary havelis with untold stories kept secret in their bosoms, among the sounds and smells of a medieval city just waking up to modernity—towards the Samriddhi Trust office, which doubled up as a workshop and a showroom. The Trust was housed in the age-old family property of Ms Singh, the force behind the organization. She was also the reason why the two friends had continued their voluntary association with the trust. Apart from literacy, education and health, the NGO worked on increasing women's incomes by providing them with skills, livelihoods, marketing, credit linkages and, most importantly, confidence. Mr Singh, they had learnt, did most of the travelling, trying to garner marketing linkages, resources and funds for the fledgling enterprises the Trust nurtured, while his wife worked on the ground to help women stand on their own feet.

Amrita taught the wards of these women—young boys and girls, who, although enrolled in the government school nearby for the sake of scholarships, free books and meals, had precious little to show in terms of actual education. Amrita realized that the children, mostly with uneducated and indifferent parents and elder siblings, had been coaxed into learning in an unfriendly environment by overburdened teachers, and found themselves alienated and miserable in the formal schools they attended. She knew they desperately needed support. It was this gap that she, along with a few other volunteers, sought to fill.

Though, for Geeta, teaching young kids often seemed monotonous, she tried to help the Trust in her own way. Being an educated engineer, she was not only good at computers but was also net-savvy, a skill that was both precious and rare at the Trust. Geeta used her skills and the tremendous powers of the World Wide Web to push the products and samples made by the women to prospective clients, who would sometimes be across oceans and time zones. As she exchanged mails with those distant clients, Geeta felt liberated, the internet providing her the escape she sought and transporting her over the morass and humdrum monotony of her everyday life. She realized that although there was satisfaction in her work at the Trust—especially when she managed to close the occasional deal that would ensure a secure income for the poor women—she felt imprisoned in an invisible cage. Geeta wondered whether Amrita, or Dinesh, ever felt like this—but then, she surmised, such thoughts were too personal to be shared even with those one believed to be closest to.

Life had not been the same since Dinesh had decided, or rather agreed, to contest the election to the legislative assembly. Dinesh wondered if it would ever be.

There were some, both within the party and without, who had wanted Dinesh to get elected to the legislative council through indirect election on the recently vacated seat. It was a safer bet and didn't involve the risk of defeat and disgrace of having been defeated from one's own father's seat. But to Dinesh's dismay, he found that Sheshmani, who had barely a couple of months back taken a jibe at those who got elected to the upper houses, was intensely lobbying to get himself elected to the legislative council on that very seat. Dinesh neither knew, nor cared why Sheshmani was suddenly so eager to join the legislature. As for himself, he was more comfortable with the idea of entering politics through direct elections, like his father had done. Dinesh genuinely believed that the upper house should be the house of elders and young politicians such as him should enter electoral politics through the heat, dust and tumble of direct elections.

'Though there are still a couple of months to go for the election, we should not waste any time or leave anything to chance. The first step is to organize booth teams—at least ten youths for each booth—and properly brief them on their duties, both during campaigning and on the day of the poll itself.' It was Yogendra talking to Dinesh above the sound of the jeep. Both of them, along with a couple of recently acquired supporters, were on their way to Barhabad, the tehsil headquarters that shared its name with that of the assembly constituency represented by Dinesh's father for three consecutive terms. Quite automatically, Yogendra had drifted towards Dinesh and had appointed himself, much to Dinesh's relief, as his principal advisor and election agent.

'Yes, I have something to go by, as this was my father's constituency, but I find that his election management was amorphous and loose. His personality and goodwill were sufficient to carry the day—but that there was never a strong, credible candidate opposite also helped,' Dinesh replied.

'Those days are gone. Politics is now a different ball game. One has to be far more organized and better managed, use more modern communication and leave nothing to chance. It is now a 24×7 occupation and amateur part-time politicians have no place in this.' Yogendra continued. 'Our opposition, too, is far better organized—it is getting significant help from some members of our own party.'

This was news to Dinesh, although, it seemed, not to the two compatriots sitting at the back of their jeep, seasoned politicians who had helped his father during his elections too. They nodded their heads, nonchalant.

'Yes, Sheshmani Pandey, through his cronies and a local moneybag called Seth Chuniram, has given money to Siddharth Goswami. Otherwise, Siddharth was in no position to contest the election. It is said that it was Sheshmani who helped the Opposition unite and decide on Siddharth as a candidate.'

Dinesh knew that Siddharth would neutralize some of the advantages Dinesh had as a candidate—he, too, was young and educated, and unlike Dinesh, didn't come from an elite background. Also, there were significant and influential Brahmin sections in the constituency. It would be a closely contested election alright.

It was almost noon when they reached the tehsil headquarters of Barhabad. Dinesh intended to meet and select his party cadres, especially his young booth teams, as well as meet some of the local influential people—religious leaders, teachers, businessmen and landed gentry. He wanted to familiarize himself with the topography of the place, the issues and problems of the people and the things that really mattered to them. He knew he must know them when the campaign started in a few days. But for Dinesh, it was much more than a mere election. He really wanted to understand the issues and problems of the farmers, so he could try and find solutions to them, irrespective of the results of the election. Dinesh wondered whether the same voters who had put so much faith in his father would believe in him and his words too. He sometimes wondered if his father's legacy was indeed an advantage, or if it would go against him, with voters feeling he was not a deserving successor.

As Dinesh moved from one youth to another, from one place to another, he couldn't help but wonder why Sheshmani was so viciously opposed to him that he had even gone to the extent of giving money to the Opposition camp.

'The real contenders in politics are almost always within one's own camp. With Opposition, one knows that the limelight and electoral success will be shared as the electoral fortunes sway over the years, but when you have a contemporary contender within your own party, he may finish your career.' Yogendra had explained it to Dinesh earlier but it was still difficult for him to comprehend such a cynical and self-centred approach to politics.

Dinesh had to admit, however, that in the case of Sheshmani, what Yogendra said was true. Dinesh had come to understand that for Sheshmani, politics and power were only means to satiate his naked and insatiable ambitions, political and otherwise. In comparison, Dinesh found his own motivations rather mild and lukewarm, as if he were in politics as a second thought, as if he had nothing better to do and that he owed his political views to others. He wondered whether he was indeed a reluctant politician, a prisoner of destiny. But then the hurly-burly, and heat and dust of electoral politics took over and he was sucked into it.

It was a late Sunday morning and although Feroze had woken up a while back to the sound of voices and clanking utensils from the open courtyard, he didn't feel like getting out of bed. It was his weekly off and he hadn't been given any special assignment by Mr Ghosh. While still lying on his cot and looking up at the white wall opposite, where a shaft of sunlight traced out a luminous circle brighter and whiter than the rest of the wall, Feroze realized that he had nowhere to go that day—and yet he felt like going out somewhere, away from home. He needed an escape. The prospect of spending the entire Sunday with his family—with his father, mother and two sisters—seemed to add to the despondency he felt in his bones.

'Have you woken up? Should I make tea for you?' It was Feroze's mother, who had peeped into his room, trying to adjust her old eyes to the dimness of the room. Feroze knew that his loving Amma had started doting even more on him since he had started earning. He knew it was not a mercenary emotion but one that had been bolstered by a rightful pride she felt in her son's achievements.

'Yes, I am getting up.' Despite himself, Feroze succumbed to the ritual of getting ready for the day. His own morning ritual lacked the namaz that was so much a part of his family members'. He didn't remember when his ways had slowly started departing from those of his family, but as far back as he could remember, he had never cared for his five namaz, nor any namaz, prescribed for a devout Muslim.

As Feroze's mother shuffled across the open courtyard to the kitchen, Feroze heard the voices of his two sisters, Fateema and Ismat, both younger than him, over the other indecipherable sounds of the lazy morning. From the snippets of their conversation that reached Feroze's ears, he could make out that they were discussing what they would like to shop for in the coming Eid festivities. As Feroze listlessly got up to go to the toilet, he felt both guilty and morose that his sisters lived in a state of suspended animation, waiting for the only eventuality of any consequence in their lives—the prospect of getting married, packed off to a similar house with a similar courtyard somewhere else, making similar conversation with their sisters-in-law or, if they were lucky, their mothers-in-law.

As Feroze came out to the open courtyard to have tea, he glanced up at the slice of sky squeezed between the parapets of the terrace. Since the monsoons had receded a couple of weeks ago, the temperature had again shot up and there was a steamy, humid edge to the September heat that was different from the dry, stark heat of May. Zaidi Saheb was sitting on his ancient armchair, looking into a distant nothingness. The armchair, just like its owner, belonged to a different era. So did the courtyard and the rooms that surrounded it. Some of them had been shuttered off years ago, having been declared beyond repair and maintenance.

Feroze realized that as soon as he had sat down on the stairs, the voices of his sisters had taken on hushed tones and the topics changed from spending and shopping to more matter-of-fact things such as dinner. Although he didn't long for his carefree childhood days when all three of them would play together in the same courtyard that now lay in front of him, Feroze felt an almost physical pang at how this insufferable and unbridgeable chasm had opened up between him and his sisters. The need for Feroze to leave as soon as possible on some pretext, any pretext, became even more urgent.

Dinesh had been keeping extremely busy in his election campaign. Perhaps, Feroze imagined, Dinesh would, at that very moment, be addressing farmers in a village or mofussil town. Feroze had once thought of accompanying Dinesh on his campaign tours—and he was sure that Dinesh would have loved his campaign to be covered in an important newspaper—but Feroze had himself felt unsure of whether he would be able to separate Feroze the journalist from Feroze the childhood friend. Perhaps he was being too conservative in his approach, he thought.

Rahul was also busy learning the ropes of being a subdivisional magistrate, or SDM, at Barabanki, and although Barabanki was closer to Lucknow than any other district, Rahul could manage to come to the capital only once in a while. To be fair, Feroze had to admit that it was always Rahul who tried to get in touch with either Feroze or Dinesh whenever he was in town.

But more than the absence of Rahul and Dinesh, Feroze knew that his sense of vacuum and restlessness that day was due to the absence of Sharmila. She had gone to Simla to present a paper at a conference of historians that was being held at the Indian Institute of Advanced Study. As Feroze sat amid the sounds, smells and sights of his childhood courtyard, among his family, he tried to imagine Sharmila walking on some tranquil mountain road, among deodars and pines, her hair ruffled by a lovely breeze. But Feroze could not do so. He had never been to any hill station, let alone to distant Simla, and it was difficult to imagine something only from bookish descriptions and second-hand tales. Feroze realized that to be missed, things had to be first lived.

And yet Feroze missed Sharmila. He didn't like to admit this solitary and hopeless emotion even to himself, and so he got up, ready to go out somewhere, anywhere, away from his family, his house, although he knew that his mother and sisters would make sure he had his breakfast first. In a way, he was glad it was so.

The government had mandated that all SDMs live at their tehsil headquarters. To Rahul's surprise, he found that none of the SDMs in Barabanki lived at the tehsil headquarters and that all of them had official houses allotted at the district headquarters, where they lived, with or without their families, and commuted in their official jeeps to the tehsil headquarters.

Much to the chagrin of older and established SDMs, Rahul had decided to live at the tehsil headquarters of Musafirabad, situated some 30 kilometres from Barabanki, towards Faizabad. He had so decided not only because it was the proper thing to do and he didn't want anybody to point fingers at him, but also because he never felt any great excitement about living in Barabanki. He would occasionally feel like visiting Lucknow, and on weekends he would often seek permission over phone from the district magistrate, Mr Arya, and head to his home city. If Rahul had been honest about his own feelings, he would have known that the real reason for him to visit Lucknow was that Rita was posted as SDM Barhabad and lived in the city itself. She had even started to consider Rahul her only friend in an otherwise new city and state.

However, Rahul had decided that he would not visit Lucknow that weekend, as he didn't think it proper to seek the DM's indulgence every time. Hence he braced himself for a solitary and hot Sunday at his official residence in Musafirabad. It was an old, somewhat neglected mansion that had come into the government's possession years ago, when the old zamindar had been almost forced to give it away on lease in circumstances forgotten in present-day memory.

Though Rahul had lived his entire life in Lucknow, he had realized only when he had started living and working in Barabanki that the mofussil towns of Uttar Pradesh, the real hinterland of the country, had a character of their own. He would not go as far as to say that these district and tehsil headquarters were crumbling away, as people of the older generation sometimes liked to imagine, but he could see the unmistakable signs that these towns were changing. The once luxuriously decorated imambaras, which, in some other place and time, would have been cherished as symbols of the nation's cultural heritage, were turning into silent, desolate sentinels of a past growing distant every day. Though the dargahs were still, especially on specific days of the week and year, bustling with people Rahul felt they laid bare the continuing insecurities of the people and their desire and compulsion to cling on to any symbol of hope. New, flashy multistorey buildings had sprung up on the crumbling facades of havelis from another era—a sign of the rising prosperity of one class and the decline of another. It was, Rahul felt, also the sign of the rise of a class of contractors—*thekedar*s. He could see them—the contractors and small-time politicians—living and operating on the borderline of law and legality, gaining influence on the formal systems of administration through the ever-expanding tentacles of an electoral politics that had become the sine qua non of modern-day democracy.

'Saheb, what would you like to have for breakfast?' Rahul's man Friday, a somewhat eccentric middle-aged man named Pitambar, asked him. Of course, Pitambar had used the word *nashta,* which could mean anything from breakfast to snacks to tiffin.

It was the first time that Rahul was staying back in his newly acquired 'home' on a holiday, and Pitambar assumed that he would want a change from his usual breakfast of paratha sabji or bread and butter that he alternated with monotonous regularity on weekdays. Rahul thought for a moment before answering. Already, he was beginning to question the wisdom of staying back that weekend.

'I will decide later. Bring me another cup of tea.' Rahul said, postponing the decision of breakfast for the moment, although it was already quite late. Maybe he would go straight to lunch, he thought.

Pitambar had barely vanished from Rahul's sight when there was a commotion outside, and neither Pitambar, nor his orderly-cum-guard, Ramlal, seemed to know how to handle it. A jeep had pulled up outside and before Rahul could fathom what was happening, Rita had stepped out of the vehicle and entered like a breeze into the office-cum-sitting room of his tehsil headquarters, pushing back the curtains and sweeping away everything and everyone in her way.

Rahul wondered at how the mere sight or presence of one person could change the very quality of the air and light around him. Suddenly the monotony and the weight of the hours that had stretched in front of him vanished and everything transformed itself, as if by magic, at the arrival of Rita, who had by then taken a chair and was looking up at him laughingly.

'They told me you were not coming to Lucknow this Sunday, so I decided to come instead.' Rita continued to laugh with her eyes. 'Uninvited, of course.'

'I am glad you did, but how did you know I was not going to Lucknow this Sunday?' Rahul was intrigued.

'I called up your home, although I think you should have told me yourself. You probably thought that it really didn't matter if I waited for you.'

Rahul wondered who would have picked up the phone at home when Rita had called. It would probably have been his father. He wondered what his father would have thought of a girl calling up and enquiring after Rahul's whereabouts. Rahul was inquisitive about what must have transpired in that conversation but was reluctant and embarrassed to admit his curiosity.

Pitambar had, for once, applied his mind and brought two cups of tea, that too on a proper tray whose presence Rahul had been unaware of till that morning.

Rita thanked Pitambar so profusely and kindly that Rahul felt ashamed at his usual insensitive behaviour towards his manservant. He could see that Pitambar was bowled over by this modern, sophisticated lady officer of the twenty-first century. Of course, Rahul knew that gossip would have already been exchanged between Rita's staff and his own, and that Pitambar would by now have known that this beautiful young woman, dressed in a dark blue suit, smiling radiantly at his saheb, was an IAS officer herself and, therefore, to be regarded as such.

'Saheb, lunch? What will you have?' this time Pitambar had decided for himself that it had become far too late for breakfast and that he might as well start preparing for lunch, as it was certain that it would now be something special. That this madam was special was written all over his saheb's face—even Pitambar could not help but notice that.

'Listen, let's go out for lunch. I saw a new restaurant on the highway that we crossed at Barabanki, which seemed nice. And then let's go to Dewa Sharif. I have heard a lot about that place and have seen the tomb of Dewa Sharif in pictures. It really looks quite impressive.' As usual, Rita had everything planned out, and Rahul could not find a single reason to object to anything.

It was still early for lunch, and Rita and Rahul decided to climb the ancient stairs of the mansion to go up to the terrace for tea. The house was, thankfully, almost on the outskirts of the rather congested town, and from the backyard of the house, they could see the countryside open up. There were stretches of emerald green paddy fields extending up to the horizon, interrupted only by the occasional mango grove, electric poles and the odd pump house. Although it was hot, there was a mild breeze; Rahul hoped that it was not particularly uncomfortable for Rita, who had been brought up in air-conditioned environments. But if she was uncomfortable, it didn't show. She was cheerful, carefree and funny, and full of stories and anecdotes about her job, her colleagues and her overly ambitious DM, who, almost a legend in the service, was trying to take her under his wing and how his jealous wife had made it clear that she didn't appreciate any special attention towards the young, female SDM.

Rahul was an attentive listener and was hanging on to every word Rita uttered, mesmerized by her ethereal beauty. Rahul was sure he had fallen in love with this desirable, yet unattainable young woman standing in front of him. He wondered whether Rita had any idea of the effect she was having on him but was sure he was not the only one who felt that way in her presence. He didn't want to read too much into Rita's driving down from Lucknow to meet him or her desire to go out for lunch and then visit Dewa Sharif. Rahul surmised that it was normal for her to behave that way with someone she thought of as a dependable friend, nothing more or less, especially when thrown as an outsider among strangers in an unknown city, state and cadre. Soon, he thought, she would get comfortable in her new surroundings and probably outgrow him.

But despite all his self-deprecating rationalisations and efforts to not get his hopes high about Rita, Rahul could not stop himself from hoping that maybe, just maybe, one day this beautiful, confident, cheerful batchmate of his would reciprocate his undisclosed feelings. After all, stranger things have been known to happen in love.

It was the first time that electronic voting machines, or EVMs, would be used in an election in India. The Election Commission of India had announced that it would use EVMs in the two by-elections first, before taking the plunge in the general elections. One by-election was in Barhabad and other in a remote constituency in Kerala.

Dinesh was taken aback when he heard about the EVMs. In private, he voiced his apprehensions to Yogendra and his close group of cadres and advisors. Even after months, Dinesh felt a slight hesitation in calling them—Yogendra, Sunil and Junaid—his friends. To him, they were political associates, close, useful and so far loyal.

'They should have experimented with EVMs in a big city first, where the infrastructure and the voters would have been better prepared for these.' Yogendra said for the umpteenth time, voicing his concern at this sudden development. None of them had even seen an EVM before, let alone use one. Even the district authorities and the polling officials were unaware of how to use an EVM; and for the thousands of voters in the hundreds of remote villages, the EVM would be an unknown and shocking installation they would face for the very first time in the loneliness of the voting chamber straight on polling day. Dinesh couldn't even imagine what the voters' reactions would be on that day!

'Whatever it be, our central leadership has given its consent to the Election Commission that it will use EVMs this by-election. Let's accept the situation and start preparing.' Dinesh knew there was no point crying over spilt milk and it was better to prepare for the eventuality.

'What do they know about the ground realities of India? All those big leaders of the Centre have not stepped out of the corridors of power and their air-conditioned rooms for ages! And it is these Rajya Sabha-type armchair politicians who are deciding the fate of the party and the nation.' Dinesh knew that whatever Yogendra said came straight from the heart; he also knew that Yogendra was right, if not wholly, then largely. But he decided to neither encourage, nor refute his colleague's remarks and let him cool down instead.

They were sitting in the large hall of the collector's office, waiting for the collector and the returning officer, who had organized a meeting of the candidates, as per the directions of the Election Commission. Siddharth, along with his supporters, had taken his place on the opposite side of the long table a few minutes back. The two candidates had awkwardly waved to one another, but their supporters had even avoided looking at each other. The meeting would have been a formal and routine affair but, with the introduction of the EVMs, there were many queries and concerns from all sides.

Dinesh saw that there were four more, non-serious candidates in the fray and that they had all come in and taken their seats. Two of them were old-time, small political pretenders who had managed to get nominations from small parties, and the other two, whom Dinesh couldn't recognize, had decided to contest as independents. Dinesh wondered if they were dummy candidates and if his own party had sponsored either of them. In the shadow and mirror world of political intrigues, Dinesh was not even sure whether they had been sponsored by somebody in his own party to help Siddharth win.

'We oppose the introduction of EVMs in this election and that, too, at this late stage. Our agents at the booth level, let alone the voters, are clueless about how to use these machines. And how do we know these EVMs can't be manipulated? After all, I myself am yet to see one. This is ridiculous!' Siddharth was vociferous in his opposition to the EVMs and was at it as soon as the collector, Kamlesh Kumar, had taken his seat and started the meeting. Dinesh knew that although he shared the same concerns as Siddharth, it would not be wise to oppose his central party leadership's consent. He also knew that the decision had already been made and opposing the inevitable would only result in distractions and appear that he was not sure of his victory.

Mr Kumar, too, agreed with Siddharth in private, but, again, was dutybound to explain how well prepared the authorities were to deploy the EVMs and what steps they were taking to familiarize the voters with the machines. In his heart, he knew that the efforts were too small and too late, but rather focused on making sure that at least the polling officials were familiar with the working of the machines. Like all 'good' administrators, he was more concerned with the 'smooth conduct' of the election, rather than its 'fairness'. He had specially deputed the bright, young IAS probationer, Rita Kaur, to lead the training of polling officials. However, although she was bright, enthusiastic and confident, she was also inexperienced, and he wondered if he had made the right choice. But then he hardly had one: his other officers, including the ADM, were both technologically incompetent and overworked.

Just as Mr Kumar was beginning to wonder why Rita was getting late, she entered the hall, along with her team of officials, who were carrying a number of EVMs. Despite being the collector, district magistrate and returning officer himself, Mr Kumar was not completely sure about how the EVMs worked and was eager to watch the demonstration.

As soon as Rita entered, pin-drop silence descended on the room and all small talk ceased. Dinesh knew that perhaps with the exception of him, Siddharth and Mr Kumar, the concerns and curiosities of all the other men in the room had all but vanished, even if temporarily. Rita's gender alone had grabbed their attention, even if they struggled against it. He didn't blame them; on the contrary, he felt bad for them, because they were prisoners of their upbringing, never having been exposed to non-relatives of the opposite gender in all the years of their lives, let alone to a beautiful, confident, urbane one. But then, he thought, maybe he himself wasn't so different from them.

As the EVM training began, both Dinesh and Siddharth had to make considerable effort to concentrate on the EVMs rather than on Rita, who was leading the demonstrations herself, instead of depending on a subordinate official. Rita, on her part, gave a fluent and effortless demonstration of how the machines worked, how they were to be 'prepared' and how the results would be stored in them and later counted. Although concerns of whether the machines were really tamper-proof and whether the voters would be able to grasp their working remained, by the end of the demonstration, everyone around the table had become reconciled to the inevitable. It was decided that during the training of the polling officials, the polling agents of candidates would also be permitted to attend the training sessions. Dinesh made a note of the training schedule and venue, and so did Siddharth. Unknown to each other, both of them decided to attend at least one of the sessions themselves.

Rita, on her part, knew that Dinesh, the candidate from the ruling party, the bright young son of the former Deputy Chief Minister who was contesting the election for the first time, was a childhood friend of Rahul's. Rahul himself had told her this as soon as it had been decided that she would be involved in the election. She also knew that Dinesh had no clue about who she was and what her relationship with Rahul was.

But, she wondered, was there indeed any relationship between her and Rahul? And was there ever any possibility of one in future? Anyway, Rita decided against approaching Dinesh during such a formal meeting and thus attract everyone's attention. She decided there would be plenty of time for that later. After all, who could tell how things would turn out between her and Rahul in the years to come—or even between Dinesh and Rahul, for that matter?

Lucknow Medical College was not Feroze's usual 'beat', but Swati, his colleague, had had to rush to Kanpur to attend to her ailing father, and Mr Ghosh had assigned Feroze to 'cover' the story. Mr Ghosh had got a whiff that an unusually high number of children, suffering from a mysterious disease, were being admitted to the ICU of the medical college for the past few days and that a couple of them had even died the previous night. He had, therefore, asked Feroze to find out what was happening.

As his colleague and press photographer Ajit navigated the Bajaj scooter through the tide of Lucknow traffic towards the medical college, Feroze, sitting on the back seat, remembered the last time he had been there on a professional assignment. It was when Raja Saheb had been brought in from an accident. That afternoon had permanently changed the course of his friend's life and perhaps that of the state politics too.

As Feroze walked up the stairs of the ICU building, he saw Dr Razdan through the glass doors. Feroze had met and known Dr Razdan on a few occasions earlier and felt fortunate that she was the doctor on duty that day. She was smart, honest, articulate and professional, and Feroze knew that he would get the facts of the case from her, without undue denial or hyperbole. Apparently, another unfortunate child had died a few minutes earlier and Dr Razdan was trying to console the poor parents while arranging for documentation formalities and the hearse. Feroze didn't want to interrupt her and, while waiting for her, tried to pick up whatever he could from the worried parents gathered there and the whispers of the staff, while Ajit took photographs. Fortunately, Dr Razdan recognized Feroze and walked up to him, perhaps to prevent him from drawing incorrect conclusions.

'What's happening here, Madam? Somebody informed us that there has been an unusually high number of children being brought into the ICU in the past couple of days, suffering from some strange disease?' Feroze asked Dr Razdan, as they walked down the newly whitewashed corridor, towards the room of the doctor on duty.

'That's true. We are still awaiting results from the laboratory, but it seems a new water-borne infection is affecting these children. All of them live in old Lucknow, and there have always been sanitation issues there. But the symptoms this time are unusual and we really can't tell for sure yet.' Dr Razdan replied. 'Of course, we are trying to do our best in the given circumstances, as you can see.'

Feroze knew that as far as Dr Razdan was concerned, there was no question of her not attempting to do everything in her power to treat her patients. He only wished he could say the same for everyone else there.

'Would it be possible to meet the chief medical superintendent or the principal of the college? I would like to take an official version from them.' Feroze asked, as they sat down on the only two chairs in the room, on opposite sides of a solitary table, on which was kept a calendar with a picture of gods and the name of a famous pharmaceutical company inscribed on it.

'Take your chance; you know the way, I am sure, to both their chambers. They may be able to shed more light on the situation than what I can provide.' It appeared to Feroze that there was a sliver of sarcasm in the last sentence, but as he looked up to check, Dr Razdan had already stood up and was giving instructions to the elderly and strict-looking head nurse, who had entered the room and was looking suspiciously at Feroze. He fancied that the nurse suspected him to be a boyfriend or a suitor of the young, good-looking lady doctor. Anyway, since Feroze was not, he had nothing more to do there and decided to 'take a chance', as Dr Razdan had suggested, with the CMS and the principal. As Feroze walked past the hushed silence in the corridors and the worry-stricken faces of burqa-clad mothers and anguished, sleep-deprived fathers, Feroze realized that almost all the families there belonged to the same locality where Feroze and his family lived. Strangely, he avoided looking in their direction, lest he recognize someone or, worse, lest someone recognize him and expect him to do something beyond his powers.

Although the CMS, Dr Yadav, was not in his room, Feroze was fortunate to find Dr Bhatia, the principal, in his huge, luxurious chamber in the more decorous administrative building of the college. Feroze was sure it was the masthead of his newspaper, inscribed on his visiting card, and not his name, that had made Dr Bhatia call him in.

'Yes, how may I help you?' The London-returned, newly appointed principal was formal and polite. Feroze had never met him before. As he explained his purpose and asked a couple of similar questions to what he had asked Dr Razdan earlier, he found Dr Bhatia, contrary to his expectations, well-informed and eloquent on the subject.

'We are yet to reach a firm conclusion about the condition these children are suffering from. It seems it has something to do with the water they drink. As you would have seen, our doctors are doing their best. There is no shortage of medicines or drugs and we are trying to provide the best possible treatment and care to them.' It was as if Dr Bhatia was reading from a script. Feroze wondered whether some of his colleagues from other newspapers had already interviewed him. He hoped not.

As Feroze settled in on the back seat of Ajit's scooter, almost on a whim he asked the photographer to head to the Jal Nigam office. The office, along with the water treatment plant and the supply system that pumped water to the older parts of the city, was situated on the banks of the Gomti River. Once they reached the shabby two-storey office building, Ajit got busy trying to capture the fading glory of the setting sun on the surface of the river. But such artistic diversions were not for Feroze and he was once again lucky that old Mr Rathee, with his paan-stained teeth and joyous manners, was present in his upper-floor office that overlooked the river. Feroze had known Mr Rathee from the days he had written the story on the increasing pollution in the Gomti River. It was the only story, Feroze still remembered with a pang of sadness, that hadn't been published in his newspaper. The regret, anger and discomfort still rankled with him. But he brushed them away and parted the grey-blue curtains to enter Mr Rathee's office. Mr Rathee was about to call it a day, but on seeing Feroze, asked the peon to bring in two cups of tea.

'Yes, what brings you here?' Mr Rathee, Feroze had known, would recognize him, although he was not sure whether he would remember his name.

'Sir, there have been a number of cases related to a water-borne disease in the old city over the past few days. I am coming straight from the medical college. I thought that since Jal Nigam supplies drinking water to that area, maybe you could throw some light on the situation.' Feroze explained.

'I can only say that our water treatment plant and piped water supply systems are working fine. Regular checks are being done and we have not found any indication of any quality issues in the water supply.'

'Maybe the pipe systems have broken down and the water is getting contaminated. After all, the systems are ancient in that part of the city and regular maintenance is non-existent, you would agree.' Feroze pressed on, as the peon brought three glass tumblers of tea and set them on the table that separated Mr Rathee from Feroze.

'I don't think so. It is the first time we are hearing of any water-borne disease. But now that you have taken the trouble to inform us, I will get it checked tomorrow—both the pipe systems and the quality of water. We have set up a swanky laboratory with World Bank money to check water quality, so we might as well put it to use. Now, have some tea.'

Feroze had noticed that the peon had brought in three tumblers instead of just two and had marvelled at his ready intelligence. Not surprisingly, Ajit entered the room with a big smile and a look of supreme satisfaction. Apparently, he had been successful in getting an excellent shot of the setting sun against the silhouette of the Chattar Manzil. Feroze couldn't help but think about how, only an hour earlier, the same Ajit had been capturing the agony and pain of helpless children and their distraught parents. He knew the daily grind of a newspaper photographer's routine had blunted Ajit's sensitivities. Feroze didn't blame Ajit—he had seen the same phenomenon in so many of his colleagues. He just hoped he would not turn out the same way someday. He feared that it was a hope in vain.

It had indeed been a long time since the three of them had met. Usually it was Rahul, whenever he was in town, who made an effort to try and arrange for a meeting. But lately, he had been engaged with his official responsibilities as an SDM and even his weekend trips to the city had become irregular.

Rahul was sitting in the newly opened first-floor restaurant, with its wood-panelled interiors and uniformed waiters, that Dinesh had suggested they all meet in. He had reached early, travelling from his sub-divisional headquarters, but was pleased to find that Dinesh had got a large, window-side table reserved for them. As Rahul settled into one of the eight straight-backed, antique-looking chairs that sat on either side of the glass-topped table and his eyes adjusted to the semi-dark interiors, he wondered whether Dinesh had invited anyone else other than the three of them. After all, this time it was Dinesh's idea to get together and celebrate his recent election victory to the legislative assembly seat.

'Some tea, coffee or lime soda while you wait for your friends, sir?' It seemed that Dinesh was acquainted with the owner of the restaurant and had spoken to him about today's engagements.

'A cup of cappuccino, please?'

As Rahul sat looking out of the large windows at the slow crawl of the Sunday afternoon traffic and the rays of the autumn sun reflected on the leaves of the tall eucalyptus trees lining the streets, he admitted to himself that the main reason for his visits to the city growing infrequent was Rita's busy schedule during the recently concluded election—Dinesh's election. It was the first successful election to be conducted with EVMs, demonstrating that the machines could indeed be used even in the interiors of a country such as India, with its numerous illiterate voters and its lack of infrastructure. Rahul wondered if Rita even realized how historic her contribution was.

'Hi.' Rita waved at him as she entered the restaurant, and as was her wont, made every neck in the sparsely populated restaurant turn, first to her and then to Rahul.

'Hi.' Rahul got up, smiling, taking Rita's confidently outstretched hand, secretly elated that it had been Rita who was the first to join him. Of course, Dinesh still had no idea that the young lady officer who had been in charge of the EVMs in his maiden election was a friend of Rahul's. It was because of this that Rahul had decided to invite Rita today as a proper occasion to introduce them. It would be quite a surprise and Rahul was eager to see Dinesh's reaction.

Too soon for Rahul's liking, though, the host arrived with Amrita and Geeta in tow. Rahul could see from the window the jalopy ease into the restaurant's parking lot. This time the manager himself, recognizing who the real VIP client was, went down to welcome Dinesh and the accompanying ladies, and escorted them up to the first floor.

Even before Rahul could react and introduce Rita to Dinesh as his batchmate and friend, Dinesh stretched out his hand towards her.

'Hi, Ma'am, I am so glad you could make it. I was hoping you wouldn't take my invitation amiss.' It was Rahul's turn to be surprised, as the amused smiles on Dinesh's and Rita's faces, and even on Geeta's and Amrita's, clearly indicated that they all shared the private joke and were enjoying the shocked expression on his own. But Rahul was indeed glad that not only had Dinesh invited Rita but also that she had accepted, despite the usual qualms that plagued the minds of officers before accepting private invitations from politicians.

As they settled in, Rahul couldn't help but observe the calm confidence that existed in the interactions, verbal and otherwise, between Dinesh and Geeta. Rahul wondered if Dinesh himself was aware of the visible chemistry between the two. It was as if somehow they 'fit together', as if they had accepted each other as natural companions. Even Amrita seemed comfortable with their chemistry. Rahul wondered if it would ever be the same for him and Rita.

Just as Rahul was beginning to wonder what was keeping their third friend, Feroze entered the restaurant. The two things Rahul noticed immediately were the bright red helmet in his hand and Ms Basu, looking as resplendent as ever in a dark green sari, who was accompanying him. As Feroze and Ms Basu settled down at the table, among greetings, smiles and handshakes, Feroze enlightened them all about the helmet.

'Lucknow has really expanded and it was getting difficult to cover so many news stories, so I decided to buy a motorbike—a Hero Honda 100. The newspaper company pays for the petrol and has advanced me an interest-free loan. I am still basically learning to ride the motorbike, but having ridden my bicycle all over Lucknow, it is not that tough,' Feroze explained. Everybody congratulated him, as it was the first time that any of them had bought a vehicle out of their own hard-earned money, even if on loan. All except Ms Basu, who seemed to not only be aware of Feroze's achievement but appeared to already have taken advantage of it, as their trip together to the restaurant that afternoon showed.

As food was ordered—naan and roti, shahi paneer and mutton korma, dal and chicken curry—the conversation began to flow in sentences and half-sentences, in laughter and interjections, interruptions and silences, and in pairs of eyes meeting and averting. Rahul wondered how that particular afternoon and its memory would play back years later. How they, in whatever circumstances they would be in then, would look back at this companionship and conversation. He fervently hoped that Rita would be there with him to share his nostalgia. It was the first time, Rahul realized, that he had permitted himself to openly hope thus.

It was as if the whole of Lucknow had been plastered with hoardings, banners and festoons to welcome Bhawani Pratap Singh on his first visit to Lucknow as the new national president of the ruling party. But Dinesh knew well that all these hoardings and posters had been put up only on the route from the Amausi airport to the VVIP guest house and nearby places by sycophantic party workers. Each one of the posters proclaimed in big, bold letters the name of the particular gentleman who had printed and put it up. Dinesh had been uncomfortable doing this but

Yogendra had insisted. Not putting up a single poster or banner by a newly elected local MLA might provoke controversy and provide an unnecessary ammunition to Dinesh's detractors within the party. So Dinesh's welcome hoarding had been put up by Yogendra at a strategic point on the route from the airport near the sugarcane research institute.

But Dinesh had not insisted on being part of the welcome team that had gone to the airport. Instead, he, along with Yogendra, had been one of the first people to reach Tilak Hall, where Bhawani Pratap was scheduled to meet his party's MLAs and other office bearers. The class IV employees were dusting, cleaning and giving final touches to the arrangements, and a couple of labourers were arranging the flower decoration on the main dais. Tilak Hall was a government meeting hall and Dinesh wondered at the propriety of arranging such a political meeting there.

'Isn't it odd that a government meeting hall, that too in the secretariat, is being used for this type of patently political meeting?' Dinesh asked Yogendra, who was sitting next to him. Both of them had settled down at one of the rows of chairs, away from but facing the dais.

'Yes, but when the chief minister himself will be sharing the dais, the difference between a political and an official meeting tends to vanish. Also, people have probably not yet realised that when Bhawaniji's father held such meetings, he was both the national president of the party and the prime minister.' Yogendra whispered, almost unnecessarily—there was hardly anybody in the hall.

It was Sheshmani who had self-abrogated the task of organizing the visit of Bhawani Pratap, and Dinesh was sure that such subtle points of Bhawaniji being party leader and not holding a governmental or constitutional post would be lost on Sheshmani; even if any of his followers pointed it out, which was unlikely, it would be brushed aside.

'Can you recognize all these people?' Yogendra asked Dinesh, pointing to the series of huge oil-paint portraits of leaders that had been a permanent fixture at Tilak Hall. It struck Dinesh that there was not a single portrait of the great Indian leader the hall itself was named after. Perhaps, he surmised, it was because Tilak belonged to Maharashtra and not to Uttar Pradesh. Silly idea, Dinesh thought.

'Most of them. But I can't recognize that old Muslim aristocratic gentleman on the extreme left,' Dinesh replied. He thought about how, over time, the importance and memories of leaders rise and fall and how their followers and supporters, with their actions or inaction, decide their fickle legacy. He wondered how his father, or he himself for that matter, would be remembered, say, fifty years later or whether they would indeed even be recognized.

There was a sudden commotion, and security men in grey safari suits and dark sunglasses, with black, handheld wireless sets and concealed weapons, swarmed the place. The front rows were quickly occupied by white-khadi-clad politicians who wanted to be seen and remembered by the young, dynamic leader. Sooner than expected, the forty-something, fair, thin-haired leader, along with the Chief Minister, burst into the hall. He was followed by a mish-mash of leaders, almost all of them much older and senior to Bhawani Pratap, who were clearly struggling to match his pace. Dinesh observed, too, that Sheshmani had taken a seat on the dais itself just next to the Chief Minister and his uncle, Vibhuti Narayan Pandey, who appeared rather subdued.

Dinesh was to learn later that Bhawani Pratap had expected the Chief Minister to be waiting on the tarmac of the Lucknow airport to receive him—something he remembered the old politician doing on his previous visits to the city with his father, when the latter had been prime minister. Bhawani Pratap had made his displeasure clear in quite a public manner on their way to the meeting hall. The manner in which it had been done had shocked and hurt the elderly man and had led to his morose mood.

The meeting was as one-sided as Dinesh could have imagined any to be: a monotonous exhorting of the ministers, MLAs and office bearers by the national president to spare no effort in making the party win the urban local body elections, and win handsomely. Although Dinesh's own constituency was almost purely rural, he had been assigned duties to work in Allahabad, especially in the university area; apparently, it was felt that he would be able to connect better with the youth. Dinesh was both eager and apprehensive. As the repetitive exhortations went on and on from the dais, Dinesh's mind began to wander.

Through the glass windows, Dinesh could see the delicious rays of the winter sun glazing the giant palm fronds and the peepul leaves. He hoped Geeta would accompany him on some of his visits to Allahabad. Of late, she had started accompanying him on some of his political tours. Initially, on a couple of occasions, Amrita, too, had travelled with them but she soon realised that political touring and campaigning were not her cup of tea. Amrita's ideals of public service were equal, if not higher, to those of Dinesh and Geeta, but Dinesh realized that it was precisely the uncompromising heights of her ideals that prevented her from being part of practical electoral politics.

Dinesh was brought back to the present with a start, as he heard his name being called from the dais. There was a beeline of politicians, who were being announced to felicitate the clearly impatient Bhawani Pratap, and Dinesh's name had suddenly been called, though he had neither shown any inclination, nor made any preparations to greet the young national president of the party. It didn't take long for Dinesh to realize that it was Sheshmani who had prompted Dinesh's name to be called, only to embarrass him, as he must have guessed Dinesh wouldn't have had one of those huge garlands or flower bouquets the other leaders were laden with. As Dinesh rose from his seat, a bouquet of fresh roses was thrust into his hands from somewhere, and as he strode towards the dais, he saw from the corner of his eyes that it had been Shiv, the police sub-inspector who had long worked as a personal security officer for Dinesh's father, who had come to his rescue. Shiv had almost snatched the bouquet from the hands of a dumbfounded leader who was waiting eagerly for his name to be called.

As Dinesh climbed the dais and handed over the fragrant bouquet to Bhawani Pratap, he sensed a fleeting pleasantness, almost relief, on the prodigal son's face, though Dinesh was meeting him for the first time. As Bhawani Pratap slowed down the proceedings to pose for the press photographers, who had just been allowed inside the hall, Dinesh realized it would be this photograph that would make it to the front pages of all local newspapers the next day. Dinesh knew that old Amzad

Sa'ab and Sharmaji of the information and public relations department would, out of a sense of loyalty to his father, make sure of this. And Sheshmani, thwarted in his efforts to embarrass him, would never realize just how much he had actually ended up benefiting Dinesh.

But Dinesh could also see that while Sheshmani was glum, his uncle's grim expression had now given way to an almost pleased look, as he was asked by the photographers to share the frame with Bhawani Pratap.

The last rays of the sun fell on the still surface of the Gomti River, as Feroze climbed up the half a dozen steps to enter the Jal Nigam office. Mr Rathee was waiting for him, as Feroze had called up beforehand. As Mr Rathee welcomed Feroze with his usual cheer, Feroze could see there was another man in the room, a small, diminutive figure wearing a dark jacket and grey muffler, sitting opposite Mr Rathee. When he, too, stood up as Feroze entered, he guessed that this man was also a government employee, but clearly junior to Mr Rathee in hierarchy.

'Hello, Ferozeji. Yes, yes, welcome. Have a seat. As you requested on phone, I have copies of the test reports—but, first of all, tell me, what will you have? Tea?' Mr Rathee was always courteous, and that evening, it appeared to Feroze he was in a particularly good mood. Without waiting for Feroze's response, Mr Rathee rang the bell and called his peon.

'Vishnu, two cups of tea. Quick.'

Feroze noticed that Mr Rathee had not offered or ordered

tea for the other man, who was busy shuffling through some papers. Feroze had decided to enquire about the results of the tests that Jal Nigam was supposed to undertake on the quality of water it supplied to the old city.

'As I told you last time, we collected samples of the water we are supplying to the old city from our pump station; we also collected samples from the taps of residents, as you had suggested last time.' Mr Rathee located the papers showing the test results and handed them to Feroze.

'As you can see, the results are quite satisfactory and the quality of water is well within the range prescribed.' Of course, it was difficult for Feroze to make head or tail of the complicated test results that had been handed to him, but he had to take them at face value. He was sure that if there had been anything amiss, Mr Rathee wouldn't have given the results to a journalist so easily.

'So the quality of water was not the real reason for the unusual disease that has afflicted some of the residents of the old city.' Feroze couldn't mask his disappointment, though he was used to chasing red herrings. Vishnu, meanwhile, had put two cups of tea and a plate of biscuits in front of them, and Feroze, despite his years of journalistic experience, felt a little embarrassed at being given such obvious preference over the other man in the room.

'Can you wait for a minute, Ferozeji? I will relieve Mr Athawale in a minute. He is the junior engineer from the electricity department and has come here on his monthly round to get his bill verified.' It was the first time that Mr Rathee had acknowledged the presence of the man, who smiled at Feroze, realizing, perhaps from the form of address Mr Rathee had used, that Feroze was an important enough man.

'Here, tell me where to sign. What is there to verify when you people do not put up a simple meter but just continue to make bills based on load? Why can't you put up a meter, so that we both know how much electricity we consume, and then pay accordingly?' All three present in the room knew that Mr Rathee didn't exactly expect any answer. The sheer lethargy, indifference and inertia of both the organisations would continue to make sure that no electricity meter was installed at the pump station.

'Sir, I am Jagdish Athawale, junior engineer at Madhyanchal Vidyut Nigam for this area. Can I have your phone number, please?' It was Feroze's turn to be surprised. It was usually the other way around—journalists asked for phone numbers of government officials. As Feroze gave Mr Athawale his mobile number, written on a chit of borrowed paper, the latter presented him with a smartly printed visiting card. Feroze suspected the junior engineer had a story to share with Feroze that he didn't want to divulge in front of Mr Rathee.

Once the junior engineer had got Mr Rathee's signatures at the desired places and bid them both goodbye, it turned out that it was Mr Rathee who had a story to tell.

'You know, Ferozeji, although our own water is perfectly fine, my team got some samples of underground water being directly pumped up by residents. Many of the residents have their own submersible pumps, in addition to our supply line, and get water directly from these on the occasions we don't supply.'

Feroze knew this, of course, having himself lived in the same neighbourhood his whole life.

'It is none of our business, really, as we are not responsible for the water we do not supply; our teams shouldn't even have collected those samples, in the first place.'

Feroze was all ears, and his brain was already racing ahead!

'The underground water that the residents are pumping themselves had peculiar pollutants, which I would say are unhealthy, even dangerous.' Mr Rathee couldn't stop himself from blurting out.

'Have you warned the people?' It was the first question that came to Feroze's mind, as the images of disease-stricken children at the medical college flashed before his eyes.

'No. It didn't concern us and it is not our supply'. Mr Rathee did not have the usual smile on his face.

'Also, I didn't want to spread panic without being sure.' Mr Rathee handed over a few loose sheets of paper to Feroze that were almost identical to the ones he had given him a while earlier. But here some of the results had been highlighted with a yellow marker. These were the test results of the samples that, Mr Rathee explained, had been taken from the water extracted by the private submersible pumps.

'What kind of pollutants are these? What can cause such pollution in groundwater?' Feroze asked the obvious question. The sun had set some time back behind a distant tomb in old Lucknow and Vishnu had re-entered the room to clear away the cups and to ask if he should light the Petromax lantern. Apparently, there was an electricity problem. Feroze realized then how dark the early winter evenings had become.

'No, Vishnu. We are just leaving.' Mr Rathee got up, indicating to Feroze that he couldn't, or wouldn't, help Feroze any further.

Although it was the second week of December, one could just about hear the faint first footsteps of the approaching winter. As the white ambassador car of Dinesh and Geeta crossed the Phaphamau Bridge over the Ganga, Geeta turned her head to the left to marvel at the gold-burnished sun taking its last bow of the day. It was as if the wide, expansive river was on fire and under her calm, resplendent surface, somewhere inside her mysterious depths, a huge cauldron had poured out lava that was floating up to the surface. At a distance, she could see a few wooden boats tied at the banks and a few village women washing clothes. In a month or so, a temporary township would appear some distance down the river, at its confluence, or 'sangam', with the Yamuna and the mythical, invisible Saraswati river, as the Ardh-Kumbh Mela would be celebrated. Dinesh could barely make out in the misty distance the initial signs of electric poles and structures being set up for the mela township.

Except the driver, Dinesh and Geeta were alone inside the speeding ambassador. Dinesh felt distracted, his amorphous thoughts swept away by the cold breeze blowing in through the half-opened windows of the car. They were returning from Allahabad, where they had gone for work connected to the urban local body election, and the incessant public work had tired their minds and pushed out all thoughts and words.

'Of late, there have been an increasing number of marriage proposals coming for me to my parents. They have been insisting that I take a look at them. I don't blame them, Dinesh, they have a younger daughter too. Naturally, my father wants both of us to be "settled" before he retires.'

It was only when she had finished her long, heavy sentence that Geeta turned to face Dinesh, looking into his eyes. Dinesh felt as if Geeta had been rehearsing the statement in her head, waiting for a suitable moment to articulate it. Although it was a statement and not a question, Dinesh knew it demanded a response. Whatever nebulous thoughts were going on in his mind vanished, as the prospect of Geeta marrying a young, eligible Kashmiri Pandit boy and perhaps leaving Lucknow, or even India, hit him.

The highway that stretched in front of them was now completely dark, penetrated only by the car's headlights. There were wheat fields on both sides shrouded in darkness and a mist lay suspended in air, as if by magic. As Dinesh looked at Geeta's beautiful face that shone through the darkness and at her luminous eyes that were still looking at him, he realized that thoughts and emotions were swirling inside his head and hammering him from inside, struggling to come out, but words were failing him. It was the first time that either of them had ever spoken about marriage. They had never even spoken about love—Dinesh, out of his fear and uncertainty about Geeta's reaction, and Geeta, perhaps out of age-old, feminine shyness, despite her modern, liberal views. Nothing had prepared Dinesh for that moment in the car, but he knew he had to respond.

Dinesh wanted to tell Geeta how much he loved her and for how long he had done so; how she had always been his centre of attraction since that day in engineering college when she had walked across the ground to his hostel. But perhaps it was the noise and vibration of the car or the presence of the driver in the front seat that prevented Dinesh from professing his feelings in such a frank manner. However, Dinesh realized that Geeta's insistent silence demanded an answer and he heard himself say, much to his own surprise: 'Will you marry me?'

He had skirted all romantic professions and come straight to the more practical issue of marriage, which was uppermost on both their minds. Love was something they had both known and accepted long back, without ever feeling the need to say it in words.

'Dinesh, there is nobody else. There has never been anybody else.' Geeta didn't answer Dinesh's question in a simple yes or no. It was not necessary. Whatever Dinesh wanted to hear had been said.

The car sped past the moffusil town of Kunda, where the highway had narrowed due to encroachments on both sides. There were some garish light decorations at an unsanitary-looking roadside eatery, in front of which a number of trucks were parked. Their ambassador had to slow down a bit.

Though Dinesh thought he would be overwhelmed by emotions and feelings at this moment they were sharing, he felt the next question, again practical, spring to his lips. 'Do you want me to talk to your parents straightaway? After all, my political career is still in its infancy and I hardly have a steady income. Besides, your family is from the educated, service class. They may have serious objections to their daughter marrying a politician, a struggling one at that.' Dinesh had wanted to add that other difference too—Geeta came from a Kashmiri Pandit family and he from a Thakur family in Uttar Pradesh—but let it be.

'There is no point in procrastinating. My parents and relatives can't understand why I am refusing to even consider any of the marriage proposals being sent by relations and friends.' Geeta replied in a clear voice, without any trace of doubt. 'If we wait for you to settle down in politics, we will both grow old and grey.' She had managed to find humour even in such a serious conversation.

'Besides, although all that you just said is true, I know my parents, especially my father, loves me too much to ever make me unhappy. Sometimes, I suspect he knows the truth and is just waiting for me to tell him myself.' Geeta had once again turned her face to look outside. The slight light that was coming in through the open window fell on her fair, delicate skin and Dinesh could barely stop himself from touching her. As the fog turned thicker, the car moved through the dark hinterland and approached an irrigation canal.

It had been three weeks since Rahul had visited Lucknow. Rita had taken a break and gone to meet 'her folks' in Chandigarh and Rahul's work had expanded to take up all his time. Now, as he drove his sky blue jeep past the Ram Sanehi Ghat and across the Indira Canal, Lucknow and its ever-expanding suburbs started creeping up on the Faizabad road from both sides. Rahul had seen Gomti Nagar come up and expand, a virtual city within a city. Here, in the newly developed parts of Lucknow, one could see wide roads, large swathes of green and signs of newly acquired prosperity—an upcoming mall, the first upmarket hotels and restaurants.

As Rahul brought his jeep to a stop in front of his home

in the government 'Bijli Colony' and climbed up the dimly lit stairs, he couldn't at first believe his ears—it was the sound of Rita's voice and sparkling laughter cascading down the gloomy stairs. Let alone introduce Rita to his parents, Rahul had never even mentioned her to them. It was not that he didn't want to but he just didn't understand what to tell them. In his own mind, there was an unspoken, unclear idea about the relationship he had with Rita. He didn't want to articulate or concretize it even in his own mind, at least, not yet.

Rahul was even more surprised when he entered his home and went up to the terrace. Apparently he had walked into an animated, light-hearted conversation: Rita was sitting with both his parents and chatting as if they had known each other for years. He noticed how achingly beautiful Rita looked, though her face was half-covered in a dupatta that she was using to avoid the direct rays of the late-afternoon sun.

'Hi, what a surprise! The son returns home!' Rita was the first to exclaim. It was definitely not a surprise to Rita, as Rahul had informed her on the phone that morning that he would come to Lucknow that evening. Rahul suspected that Rita was mocking Rahul's own surprise by feigning hers. There were three empty cups of tea on the small centre table that had been brought up from the drawing room. Mr Srivastava was sitting on his usual chair and both Rita and his mother were sitting on string settees that had been placed around the low table. Rahul couldn't remember the last time he had seen his mother so resplendently happy and content. Even when Rahul had passed the civil service exams and it was clear to everybody that he would soon become an IAS officer, it was

Rahul's father who had been more visibly happy.

'We were discussing your childhood days and how Lucknow has changed over the years and how it used to be so much greener.' Rita said, looking up at Rahul, even as the latter tried to make sense of why, how and when Rita had come home, and how she had made the conversation and companionship with his parents so natural. He wondered what his own parents were thinking of this vivacious, sweet-talking, modern girl.

'Will you have tea?' Rahul's mother had got up, silently pushing her own settee towards her son and making a hesitant move towards the kitchen that adjoined the terrace.

'No, no, you sit, I will get another settee.' Rahul really wanted his mother to stay, not for himself but for her. It was so rarely that he saw his mother sitting contently, looking relaxed, happy and comfortable, without the ever-pressing thought of the next chore, the next meal, the next responsibility.

'Yes, Aunty, do sit. We'll go and make some tea.' Rahul was even more flabbergasted at Rita's suggestion. He even felt that she was going a little overboard—after all, it was her first visit to his home. To suggest that she would go to the sacred hearth of his mother's home to make tea for them seemed a bit too much. But to his surprise, neither of his parents seemed to mind and, to Rahul's amazement, his mother sat down again as Rita got up and headed to the kitchen. Although Rahul had no idea how to make tea, or anything for that matter, he had no choice but to follow her.

The tiny, dingy kitchen had been half the world for his mother since she had entered the house as a young bride more than two decades ago. The roof and the walls that were once white were now covered with a thin film of accumulated cooking oil, grime and soot; the rows of plastic jars that contained a variety of spices and condiments; the ancient-looking gas burner; and the tiny, tired exhaust fan—all appeared even more oppressive and claustrophobic to Rahul. Maybe because it was the first time he was seeing somebody other than his mother in the kitchen. He realized how much he had taken her for granted.

'When did you come? And how are you here?' The two questions tumbled out.

'I thought you were never going to introduce me to your parents, so I took the lead. After all, how long could I wait? And, as I realized on this trip home, how long could I expect my parents to wait?' Rita replied, looking straight at the water she had put on the gas stove to boil. Almost effortlessly, she had found the exact location of the Brooke Bond tea leaves, the sugar and the milk.

Rahul couldn't see the expression on Rita's face as it was turned away from him, but though his rational mind knew there could only be one purport of Rita's words, his heart was still sceptical, not wanting to jump to conclusions.

Yes, they had indeed grown close since they had left the academy and landed up in the same state, and although Rahul knew how his heart missed a beat every time he saw Rita, he was afraid to imagine that the vivacious girl standing in his kitchen that very moment could ever consider him good enough. And yet what Rita had uttered just minutes ago could only mean one thing.

In that magical moment, as the truth and import of Rita's words began to sink in, Rahul felt like putting his arms around her and pulling her to him. It was not the first time he had wanted to do so but it was the first time he had felt that his secret desire could become a possibility. But that was not to be, as Rita had already picked up the tray, with four cups and a pot of tea balanced on it, and turned to look at him. Rahul could see that she was serious and the spontaneous mirth in her eyes had given way to something deep and molten. The moment to hug her had passed but it had transformed into one of complete understanding between them, where no talk, no hug, no physical touch was any longer necessary.

Lately, Feroze had been wondering whether it was at all possible for him to pursue his doctoral studies along with his professional work as a full-time staff reporter, with its long and uncertain work hours. One of his colleagues had recently been forced to quit, thanks to the company's relentless pursuit of profitability by cutting costs and increasing advertisement revenue, and most of that unfortunate colleague's beat had landed up on Feroze's lap. Moreover, he had been feeling that the subject of his PhD thesis, which was naturally guided and suggested by Sharmila, was too ambitious. It was related to the effects of international geopolitical events on the Indian national movement. This was one aspect of the Indian freedom movement that Feroze felt was not explored in standard school, or even college-level, textbooks. Feroze had to admit that the subject was revealing and intellectually stimulating. And yet, Feroze was getting increasingly frustrated at his inability to devote sufficient time to his research work. Sometimes, on days such as this one, he even wondered whether he was continuing with his academics only to find an excuse to keep in touch with and enjoy the company of Sharmila.

As Feroze pushed open the half-broken, iron grill gate of Sharmila's university-provided house and proceeded towards the main door to ring the bell, he felt that familiar breathlessness and quickening of pulse at the prospect of meeting her. He knew his attraction towards Sharmila was one that had no hope or future and yet he couldn't deny himself this temporary, yet futile self-indulgence.

She was dressed in a beautiful blue silk saree and had put on some make-up. She appeared to be especially resplendent and luminous as she opened the door that day. Usually, it was Bala who opened the door when Feroze came to meet Sharmila.

'Hi, were you going out? You should have told me.' Feroze didn't want to disturb Sharmila's plans but he had rung up before starting for her place to let her know he would be coming.

'I am telling you now. I am indeed going out.' Sharmila was all laughter and fun that evening and though Feroze was puzzled at this strange change of behaviour from her usually serious and sober self, he couldn't help notice how beautiful she looked in such a mood. 'But I am going out with you.' Sharmila led him to the drawing room and sat down on one of the wicker chairs. This, too, was unusual, as, whenever Feroze came over to study, they would sit on the chairs around the dining table, which would have books, papers, journals and notebooks strewn around. But that day, the table had been cleaned up and so had the entire drawing-cum-dining room. The only light came from a beautiful lamp that Feroze had not noticed earlier.

Feroze sat down tentatively, not knowing the cause behind Sharmila's unexpected happiness, but he was glad. Though he didn't say anything, there was a question on his face.

'Why, don't I have the right to feel happy? Don't I have any right to go out with you?' It was as if she was both mocking and daring Feroze.

'Of course you do. I only wish you were like this more often. But may I know the reason?'

'Do you remember that paper I had been writing for some time? It has been accepted by the Indian Council of Historical Research and I have been invited to present it at their annual conference.'

Feroze knew about Sharmila's paper. Indeed, he had helped her collect relevant source material from various libraries and archives. It helped him too, as her paper was on the so-called 'Great Game', the international espionage and counter-espionage practised by the British and the Russian empires in Central Asia and Tibet during the nineteenth century. It was something that was related to, even if distantly, to Feroze's own PhD thesis.

'That's really great news! Where and when is the conference?'

'It is in Simla, at the Indian Institute of Advanced Study.' Quite appropriate too, Feroze thought, as he knew that the venue had been the viceregal lodge of British India's summer capital, from where many of the plans and strategies of the Great Game may have been drawn.

'I am, like the other invitees, being offered two to and fro tickets. Can you come with me? After all, you did help me a lot in writing the paper.' Sharmila was now directly looking at Feroze, the lamp shade casting a shadow on half her face.

'That help was nothing. Any of your students would have done that.' Feroze would have loved to accept Sharmila's invitation; a journey with her up to the imagined beauties of the Himalayas was the stuff of dreams for him, though he had had neither the time, nor the opportunity to dream about anything so remote. And yet he didn't want to go merely because he had helped her in her paper.

'Forget that. Can you come with me, just like that, for once? It would be very nice. Can you please take leave from your office, for once, for my sake? Can you please give your family some excuse that I can't think of?' Her eyes and voice were pleading, and all the joyful mirth of only a few moments ago had turned into something deeper.

Feroze felt as if he was being sucked into a whirlpool of joy. Though his mind and common sense were telling him there could never be any future for him, a lower-middle-class Muslim boy from a deeply conservative family, and this modern, Westernized, Hindu woman who was both a divorcee and older to him, Feroze couldn't bring himself to refuse. It would have been too cruel—both to her and to him.

It was one of those large bungalows that the Public Works Department had built for its senior officers. It was situated at the edge of Dilkusha Colony. Just beyond the colony was dense wilderness, and perhaps because most of these swathes were defence estates, the city hadn't spread out in this direction. Hence Dilkusha Colony and the Nawabi-era Dilkusha Kothi nearby, from which the colony derived its name, appeared to be more distant and remote from the city than they actually were. It was this bungalow that Mr Zutshi, Geeta's father, had been allotted when he was promoted to chief engineer, and it was here that Geeta lived with her parents and two younger siblings.

Though Dinesh had prepared himself before arriving, he still felt some trepidation and anxiety as he announced his arrival to the peon who opened the main door. Geeta had already told her family of her intention to get married to Dinesh but had also impressed upon her parents that their, especially her father's, opinion and consent were important to them. Apparently, neither had the news come as a great shock to them, nor had they flown into a rage. In fact, it was Geeta's parents who had suggested that Dinesh come to their place one evening for tea.

As Dinesh settled down on one of the sofas in the tastefully designed drawing room, he realized it had been especially done up to welcome him, just like he had made sure he was particularly presentable that evening.

Soon, Mr Zutshi joined Dinesh and, as if to check how the two men got along, Geeta joined them. Dinesh and Mr Zutshi had met at official and semi-official functions before, both during Raja Surendra Singh's time as minister and later, when Dinesh became a member of the legislative assembly himself. But that evening was neither official, nor semi-official and demanded a different tone of conversation. Quite a long time was spent talking about seemingly neutral, innocuous things such as the weather, politics and even cricket, before either could dare to turn the conversation to the subject they both wanted to talk about. It was Dinesh who decided to take the initiative.

'I can understand your position, sir. Geeta must have told you about our wish to marry but, frankly, as I told Geeta too, my career and prospects in politics are uncertain and can be quite unsteady in terms of money.' Dinesh felt that rather than convincing Mr Zutshi, his words were dissuading him. And yet he felt that he should tell them the things that he really, honestly felt. He was sure, from what Geeta had told him, that Mr Zutshi, like Dinesh himself, had Geeta's best interests at heart.

'But I can also say, sir, that I treasure Geeta and will do whatever I can to keep her happy. Though I don't claim that I can ever fully make up for all the love and affection she has got from you and your family, I feel she will be happiest with me.' If Dinesh's earlier words of caution were honest, this came straight from his heart, without any rehearsal or practice. Without actually asking for Mr Zutshi's permission, he had said whatever needed to be said.

It was at this moment, just before Mr Zutshi's response, or verdict, was expected, Geeta's mother entered the room and took her place. The need for polite greetings and pleasantries dissolved the suspended tension in the room and yet Dinesh was impatient to hear what the patriarch had to say. Thankfully, it was not too long before Mr Zutshi returned to the point where the conversation had paused.

'We may appear to be a typical service-class Kashmiri Pandit family but I am the first in our extended family to be part of a regular job. We are a family of lawyers who have lived for more than two generations in Allahabad and, as you would know, in that city, in the good old days, all lawyers were somewhat political, even if not full-time politicians.' Mr Zutshi had a way of conversing that was unhurried and comforting at the same time. At least, he is not disturbed or angry, Dinesh thought.

'Politicians from the days of Jawaharlal Nehru have visited our house, even during Rajiv Gandhi's time. I myself had been obliquely offered a place in the party and had even been requested to contest from the Yamunapar seat.'

'Then what happened? Obviously, you refused.' Dinesh was curious and yet felt that Mr Zutshi was trying to convey, in an indirect way, that Dinesh's being in politics would not go against him.

'I have a lot of respect for your father, who was our departmental minister. He understood things and was open and sensible. I was so sorry to hear about his accident. Please convey my regards to him.'

Yet again, Mr Zutshi was not answering Dinesh's question directly. But then Dinesh realized that he hadn't asked him a direct question either.

'Sir, will you and Aunty agree to give your consent and blessing to our marriage?' This was about as direct as Dinesh could get.

This time it was Mrs Zutshi, of clear, translucent skin and beautiful, clear eyes, who spoke before Mr Zutshi could say anything.

'For us, our daughter's, our children's, happiness has always been the most important. I only wish that you have the strength to stick to the path of right, moral politics and not get sucked into the ills so many politicians succumb to. That is the reason why Siddharth, Mr Zutshi, had declined from joining politics. He was not sure if he would be able to stick to the narrow and straight path. I wish you do, for your sake, for Geeta's sake and for everyone's sake, because I know that if you ever do swerve from that path, Geeta will never be able to find happiness again. She may remain with you out of her love for you, but she will lose herself. Please, never let her lose herself, beta.' It was the first time she, or anybody in the family, had addressed Dinesh as beta. It was also the first time, Dinesh later realized, that anybody other than his late mother had addressed him as such.

A cool breeze had started blowing outside and light, wispy cotton from the red silk cotton tree had floated in through the large, open bay windows. Dinesh had believed since he was a child—one of those irrational, inherited beliefs—that if you caught one of these and made a silent, secret wish, it would come true. Dinesh wanted to catch one now but let it go.

His wish had already come true.

Feroze and Sharmila had decided to take the overnight Chandigarh Express and then drive on to Simla. For the first time, Feroze had decided to lie to his family but knew it was necessary, not for him but for them. He knew that his simple parents would never enquire why Feroze was required to travel to Simla for a special reporting assignment, when the national newspaper already had a full-fledged bureau office in Simla. Instead of joining Sharmila at the Charbagh station where the journey was to start, Feroze had packed a few mild woollens into his old leather suitcase and walked to the Lucknow city railway station that night. It would have been impossible for him to explain to his family why he needed to travel for miles in the opposite direction to Charbagh junction when its very next stop, the Lucknow city station, was a stone's throw from their home.

As Feroze waited at the almost deserted station, he asked for a jodi of saada paan and a 'loose' cigarette—a recent habit—from the paanwalla plying his trade just outside the platform. Memories of his many childhood journeys came unbidden, when they as a family would board the train to their mother's native village in Pilibhit from this very station. It was an obscure metre-gauge railway line, the 'choti line', in common parlance. The train was even more obscure, a relic of the Awadh-Rohilakhand railway company days. They would always travel second class, with its wooden berths and shuttered windows—and yet how happy and hopeful they had been! Zaidi Saheb was still earning well, his maternal grandparents were still alive and relatively prosperous in their village, and their ancient, inherited farms produced enough money. The despondency and hopelessness of the later years were yet to seep in. But it was maybe memories of those happy times that made the present appear even more sad and oppressive to Feroze. He wanted to spit the memories out like the betel juice that had filled up his mouth, but he knew there was no escaping the gloominess he felt—it had seeped into his bones. Fortunately, the piercing whistle and headlight of the approaching Chandigarh Express jolted him out of his reverie, as he rushed to identify and then board the AC II coach.

Sharmila had already procured from the coach attendant the white bedsheets, or rather berth sheets, pillows and blankets for Feroze, and was waiting, radiant and happy, like a schoolgirl on her first school trip. Looking at her so happy, as she had been from the time Feroze had agreed to travel with her, made Feroze both happy and hopeless at the same time. To find someone he loved so happy and to know that he was the reason behind it felt like liquid warmth inside him, and yet the utter hopelessness of their situation struck him like a hammer blow every time he thought about it.

'We are in luck. The other two berths seem to be empty.' Sharmila said, as Feroze struggled to push his suitcase under the berth, adjusting her luggage that was easily twice as much as Feroze's.

'I don't think so. I just caught a fleeting look at the reservation chart as it was being pasted on the coach—there are no empty berths. Unless they have decided to miss the train, they will be here any second. It is only a two-minute stop.'

Just then there was a minor commotion and an officious looking peon wearing a brass plate and a rather fanciful cap, along with a uniformed home guard, entered their coupe. There was a thin, emaciated coolie in a red shirt carrying luggage just behind them. The two occupants of the remaining berths appeared to be government officials.

For both Feroze and Sharmila, Rita's arrival came as a pleasant surprise but it was even more shocking when Rahul entered the coupe to occupy the fourth berth. Even for Rahul, finding Feroze and Sharmila there was nothing short of amazing, as he could never have imagined his childhood friend, who never went anywhere, travelling to Chandigarh with Ms Basu, most certainly clandestinely. Rahul himself had decided to accompany Rita to Chandigarh to meet her parents. That all four of them had found themselves on the same train in the same coupe was a happy coincidence for all of them. They soon settled down to the comfort of familiar and friendly company, as the train left the sprawling suburbs of Lucknow and entered a world of darkness where a light mist hung over invisible fields.

It is very often that such journeys provide the time and space for thoughts to crystallize and, in the presence of easy, intimate company, such thoughts, hopes and longings take the shape of words that come out with effortless fluidity. This was one such journey.

It was Rita who spoke first. The normally effervescent and gregarious girl was sober that night, as if the turbulent waves of an ocean after a storm had calmed down.

'In Mussoorie, Rahul was one of my many batchmates and friends. Many of the boys tried to approach me, some made it amply clear that they fancied me, a couple of them even formally proposed to me. It was not that I was averse to the idea of marriage, and my parents were particularly keen that I "find" a suitable partner in the academy itself, but none of those boys really appealed to me.' Rita was in a mood to unburden herself and the other three in the coupe were eager, understanding listeners. Rahul knew some of the boys Rita spoke about. 'Rahul was never one of them. He was always polite and correct, and though I suspected he liked me and my company, he would never show it and would even go to great lengths to keep things civil and formal.' Rita was smiling as she remembered those days.

'Rahul may not have broken through his barriers and told you how much he loved you but I am sure you could see it plainly. Women have a way to tell when a man is seriously fond of them.' Ms Basu responded with equal honesty and earnestness.

Feroze was not completely sure whether Sharmila was alluding only to Rahul's feelings for Rita or whether she meant something more, about Feroze's carefully wrapped-up feelings for her. He suspected that she meant both. He merely kept quiet and let the conversation flow, as the train continued to hurtle through the opaque darkness of the surrounding countryside that was only occasionally broken by clumps of electric light that represented small habitations fortunate enough to have them.

'I may not be the best person to advise you on marriage, as my own ended in bitter failure, but sometimes failure teaches you more than success. Rita, I can see that Rahul loves you very much and very sincerely, and I have seen enough of him in the past couple of years to recognize that. You are indeed a lucky girl to have someone love you with such transparent honesty. When it comes to marriage, I can tell you one thing: always marry someone who loves you, rather than one whom you think you love.'

For a moment, Feroze thought that perhaps Sharmila would, for the first time, delve into the story of her own marriage and how it had failed, but she was not ready yet to show them her past, her wounds. Perhaps the wounds, carefully bandaged over, were still raw and painful, Feroze thought.

'We are going to meet my parents to try and convince them to give their blessings to our marriage, and ask to get it arranged. But I know my parents. I am afraid it is almost impossible that my father will agree to our proposition. His ideas of suitability are so entrenched in ideas of caste, religion, region and status that I don't see him agreeing. Though my mother loves me and would love to agree with me, she won't dare go against the domineering will of my father.' Rita was talking to them and yet it appeared as if she was speaking to herself, trying to collect her thoughts before she actually faced her parents.

'So if your fears do indeed come true—though I hope they don't—and your father doesn't see reason, what will you do?' This time it was Feroze who asked the question, looking at Rita and then to Rahul, who was sitting on the opposite berth.

'I am not ready to give up my life, my happiness and my love for the sake of some wrong, fanciful ideas that my father has, that's for sure. My father will never give his consent to my getting married to anybody other than a rich, Punjabi boy. It is only on Rahul's insistence that we try and ask for his consent that we are going to Chandigarh. I do not fear the eventual consequence but I do fear the mess, the emotional blackmail and prejudiced rudeness that may crop up in the interim. I don't think I am acting selfishly by living my life as per my values and choices. If at all, it is my father who is acting selfishly by wanting me to live my life as per his wishes.'

It was precisely at this moment, before either Ms Basu or Feroze could say anything in response, that the train eased itself into a half-asleep but brightly lit railway station. There was some commotion as waiting passengers and large families got into the carriage and a few disembarked. It was well past midnight but even at such a late hour, there were tea vendors plying their trade.

As Feroze looked out the window, he couldn't help thinking about those dark, sinewy men and their families, and what kind of economic compulsion forced them to stay away from their home and hearth at such ungodly hours. Looking at the poor, miserable creatures of the railway station—vendors, the destitute sleeping on open platforms, beggars and drug addicts—Feroze felt as if his own despondencies, sorrows and anxieties, those of Rahul's and Rita's, and others like them, were embarrassing self-indulgences. From somewhere in his distant past, a line from an Urdu couplet floated up: "*Aur bhi dukh hai zamaane mein mohabbat ke siwa*..." There are other sorrows in this world other than those of love...

The conversation had reached its natural end, as the train came to a halt with almost a violent lurch, and the outside world came rushing in through the open windows, breaking their intimate isolation of just a few minutes ago.

Dinesh had never been able to fully understand why Sheshmani was so viscerally opposed to him. At every opportunity, he seemed to be doing everything possible to sideline and isolate Dinesh. Sheshmani's physical closeness to the Chief Minister, who was also the president of the state unit of the party, and his apparent influence on his uncle's decisions had given him a clout within the power structure of the century-old party that couldn't be justified by his just being a member of the legislative council.

Dinesh had never noticed the games that Sheshmani played to thwart any chance of Dinesh's political ascendancy;

it was Yogendra who alerted him to how the crafty politician was slowly making sure that Dinesh had no role to play in the organisational structures and decision-making bodies of the party. Whenever an opportunity arose of nominating someone from the ruling party to an office of patronage, Dinesh's name would be kept strictly out of the reckoning. Unlike Dinesh, however, Yogendra had a ready explanation for why Sheshmani did what he did.

'He is looking at the future. He knows that after 10 years or so, when his uncle is no longer around, you will be one of the most important contenders for the party's leadership. Naturally, he is making sure that is not going to be the case; he is making the party cadres understand that it is with him, and him alone, that their futures lie. With leaders of other political parties, you merely take turns to be in the government and in the Opposition. But the real battles for political supremacy are always fought within one's own party.' Yogendra had said this before to Dinesh.

The two, along with Geeta, were on their way to Dinesh's constituency and had stopped at a roadside eatery. It was a clean dhaba run by an ex-army man and had, because of its location, service and quality of food, made a name for itself in recent years. Dinesh realized, not for the first time, that Yogendra, with his years of politics at the booth level, had an earthy wisdom and an ear to the ground that was invaluable to Dinesh. He was grateful that he had at least Yogendra with him, a selfless, hardworking loyalist who was not afraid to speak even unpleasant truths to his face.

'That seems to explain a lot. But what Sheshmani has most purposefully done is block your access to the Chief

Minister, because he knows that the old man, because of his past association with your father, and otherwise, likes you and tends to listen to you.' It was Geeta this time, nodding her head in agreement to Yogendra's theory. Dinesh had to admit that Geeta, despite having no political background, had already acquired quite a bit of political acumen, especially since they had decided to get married. It had been at Geeta's family's insistence that the marriage ceremony was scheduled for the coming November, which was still some months away.

It was well past 2 p.m. and Dinesh had ordered lunch for all of them, including the driver and the gunner, who sat at a separate table. Soon a simple but sumptuous meal of hot chapatis, dal tadka and mixed vegetables, along with pickles, onions and papad, were brought to their table by a scrawny village boy.

'You may be right, but why would Sheshmani single me out as his potential political contender? There are many other MLAs and leaders in the party.' Dinesh knew that Yogendra was perhaps largely right but, still, his theory didn't seem to be able to explain fully the ruthless opposition that Sheshmani had started displaying towards him. More than opposition or competition, it was an almost inexplicable, cold hatred that seemed to lurk somewhere behind Sheshmani's smile whenever they met.

'You underestimate yourself. Your legacy, your education, your eloquence, your caste and, above all, your age makes you one of the most dangerous contenders Sheshmani will have in future—and Sheshmani knows that. He will go to any lengths, and I mean any, to see that there is no obstruction to his smooth progression to becoming chief minister of the state in the coming years. He is a 24-hour full-time politician, unlike you.' Yogendra had already polished off two chapatis and ordered more dal as he started on his third. By this time the owner of the dhaba had come to know that the local MLA was at his eatery and had come to ask after them.

The dhaba owner, Subedar Sushil Maurya, had switched on the TV, perhaps especially for them, and had put on one of the 24-hour private news channels that had come up recently in India after the advent of satellite TV. There was a heavily made-up young woman wearing a Western suit excitedly gesticulating and saying something in a high pitch. Dinesh could barely make out what she was saying, but the fast-moving red-and-yellow 'ticker' at the bottom of the screen showing 'breaking news' caught his attention. For once, 'breaking news' was actually something that was shockingly important, at least to them.

It seemed that the young national president of the party had given an exclusive interview to the channel a couple of hours ago and had, among other things, announced the unprecedented policy of 'one man, one post' in the party. Since then, wide speculations had erupted in political circles and news channels about what it meant: who were the people holding more than one post and if they were indeed asked to give up the extra posts, who would be the likely candidates to take them up?

As the three sat stunned, trying to make sense of the announcement—its possible cause and probable implications for their state—its full import began to take shape in their minds. Inevitably, it was Yogendra who spoke first, as soon as the news bulletin was interrupted by an advertisement break.

'Sheshmani will now have to make sure that he becomes the state president of the party, as Pandeyji will have to vacate the state party president's post. Ideally, Sheshmani would have liked to wait a few more years, until he had gained complete control of the party apparatus, but knowing him, he will not give up this chance and will move heaven and earth to become the next president.' Dinesh knew that Yogendra was right and realized that once Sheshmani had indeed taken over as state party president, he would not only make sure Dinesh's political career was over but also that his own sycophantic acolytes manned every single post within the party's hierarchy. Suddenly, all the future battles of contention and political intrigue stood staring them in the here and now. Perhaps that was exactly what the national president wanted, Dinesh thought. If anything, inconsistency and unpredictability were the two most essential qualities of a politician. It made sure that one's opponents were always on their toes, reacting rather than preparing. In addition, it made sure that one was always in the news. Dinesh had come to realize how many politicians of his generation—those who had come of age in the era of 24-hour news channels—would go to any extent to stay in front of the camera, in the news, for whatever reasons, good or bad; it was considered worse to be forgotten, to vanish from public memory, than to be in the news for the wrong reasons.

'Yes, but won't the older leaders revolt? Will they accept Sheshmani's leadership?' Geeta asked. Her question was only natural, but both Yogendra and Dinesh knew that the real question in the coming days would be who had more money and the bigger numbers, and invariably—and unfortunately—in the murky, amoral world of politics, the latter was often decided by the former.

At first, Feroze didn't recognize the short, bespectacled man wrapped in woollen mufflers standing in front of him. He wore a heavy, shapeless cap and was unmistakably smiling at him. Feroze didn't mind either not recognizing or being recognized, in fact even welcoming the latter on this three-day break with Sharmila in Simla. The two of them were enjoying a long, leisurely walk early in the morning on the roads that wound up and around the mountains, opening up fine vistas of hamlets and terraced fields. Sharmila's paper had been received very well the previous day. The pointed and well-informed questions from her peers in the audience had been answered with a mix of erudition and eloquence by her that had only increased her estimation in Feroze's eyes. Today the schedule was comparatively light and Sharmila had wanted them to go for a long walk from one end of Simla, where the Indian Institute of Advanced Study stood, to the other—past the Ridge, the Mall, the iconic Gaiety Theatre, the Town Hall, Christ Church and Hanuman temple, all those sights that were best enjoyed in the early morning before the hustle-bustle of the day changed the city from a colonial capital to a modern moffusil town.

And now, as they reached what was called the 'Scandal Point', this smiling man swathed in woollens and greetings, forced Feroze to halt their walk. But the moment the stranger removed his cap, first looking at Feroze and then at Sharmila, recognition dawned on him. The changed setting and complete unexpectedness of the meeting had led Feroze to not recognize Mr Athawale, the junior engineer from the state electricity department in Lucknow whom he had met at the Jal Nigam office only a few days back.

'Pranam, Feroze Sa'ab. What a pleasant surprise to find you here.' Mr Athawale greeted Feroze without any hint of irony.

'Hello, Athawaleji, on holiday here in Simla?' Feroze had enquired innocently enough, but the answer was apparently not so straightforward, as was borne out by Mr Athawale's visible uneasiness and hesitation. Maybe he was actually there on an inspection visit to the factory premises of one of the electrical equipment suppliers—a lot of such factories had been set up near Simla in the last few years to get tax advantage of the government's policies that encouraged setting up industries in the hills. Maybe the supplier company was financing Mr Athawale's inspection visit, and by extension his family vacation. Whatever it be, Feroze realized he shouldn't have asked this question and embarrassed Mr Athawale, especially in the presence of his family.

Feroze could see over Mr Athawale's shoulder a plain looking, middle-aged woman and a teenage boy approaching them. Clearly, Mr Athawale was accompanied by his wife and son, and Feroze hoped they would be glad to cut short the greetings and resume their walk to wherever they were going.

'Meet my family—my wife and my son, Prateek. He studies in Class VIII in St Francis.' Mr Athawale was beaming with pride at the mention of his son and even more at the mention of the old, prestigious convent school in Lucknow where his son studied. It was something that Feroze had observed in many middle-income, aspirational families. Both his wife and son greeted Feroze and Sharmila with folded hands and polite smiles. If Mr Athawale was expecting Feroze to introduce Sharmila in a similar manner, his disappointment didn't show. Feroze knew that Sharmila must have ignited some curiosity in Mr Athawale and that he must have been trying to place this beautiful, early-middle-aged, Westernized lady in smart track suits and with open, lustrous hair into some acceptable category, some bracket. But Feroze was thankful that at least Mr Athawale was discreet enough to conceal his excitement.

'Feroze sa'ab, I won't detain you, but can you please come and have tea with me anytime during the day? I want to talk to you about something, something important. The fact that I am meeting you here, in Simla of all places, makes me believe that destiny wants me to speak to you.' Mr Athawale's countenance had undergone a change and he was now looking up at Feroze with a seriousness that was lined with hope and eagerness. Although Feroze understood that Mr Athawale was keen to share with him some material he believed to be news-worthy and though professionally he was inclined to take up the offer, he had to remind himself that he had indeed come on a well-earned, duly sanctioned leave, that too with Sharmila—something that was unlikely to be repeated too many times in his life, in their lives. But before Feroze could overcome his hesitation and mouth a polite, socially acceptable refusal, Sharmila, who had been silent all this while, spoke up.

'Sure, Feroze should be able to make it. I will be busy at the conference, and he can stop at the mall on our return and you two can have some chai-shai at one of the cafés on Mall Road. In fact, I know of a cute little place right opposite the Town Hall. They have lovely cakes and, though it can be a little cramped, it provides excellent views of the valley and is good value for money.' Sharmila had, in one flourish, sealed everything; after that, Feroze could no longer have anything more to say. Mr Athawale was, of course, beaming and thanking her profusely.

'Thank you so much, Ma'am. Thank you so much. It is very convenient too. Our hotel is right next to Mall Road. So Feroze sa'ab, I will wait for you there at, say, 10 o' clock?'

Feroze could only nod in agreement. Mr Athawale and Sharmila had, between them, decided the course of his morning. When they had started on their walk that morning, Feroze had had no idea that it was going to unfold in such a fashion. But then he quickly realized that it was like that all the time. Even a few days ago, he had no idea that he would be enjoying such an exclusive, albeit unadmitted, intimacy with Sharmila in such beautiful and even romantic climes. Life, thought Feroze, was like a mountain road, and nobody knew what view the next turn would bring.

And so Feroze was to realize again in the next couple of hours, when he faced Mr Athawale on the open terrace of Café Moonlight. Feroze had had to crouch low while climbing the cramped wooden staircase of the café, taking care not to bump his head on the low ledge above, wondering how taller people ever managed. However, the beautiful, sun-drenched views that the terrace afforded, the cool, crisp breeze, the delicious smell of freshly brewed coffee and the exotic-looking cakes on display in the glass counter all appeared to be compensation enough. All the tables on the terrace were occupied. True to his word, Mr Athawale was already there waiting for Feroze, and had, to his delight, chosen the table that overlooked the valley.

That the man had a keen eye not only for such matters but a perceptive and discerning mind concealed beneath his plain demeanour was to be obvious to Feroze soon after, as the junior engineer started to speak, revealing the reason why he had been so keen to meet the young correspondent of the most widely read newspaper in India.

As Rahul and Rita had feared, Rita's father, Sardar Tejveer Singh, retired chief secretary of Punjab, was not open to even considering marriage between them. Though he loved his only daughter and had done everything to make her childhood and upbringing comfortable, his inherent prejudices and mental barriers ruled out any prospect in his mind of his children marrying outside the Sikh and Punjabi community.

'Listen, Rita has found someone from her own batch in the IAS and in the same cadre, a boy named Rahul…' It had been up to Rita's mother to break the news to her husband, not because Rita was shy or fearful of broaching the subject, but because her mother thought it would be better, more peaceful and possibly even successful if she, his partner for over 25 years, did so. But even she had agreed that both Rita and Baldev, her elder son, should be there to accompany and fortify her. If the Sardarni had thought they would be better off if she broke the topic, she was mistaken. Her husband didn't even let her finish.

'The question doesn't even arise of anyone other than a Sikh to enter this house as my son-in-law. I am aware that there is a Sikh boy in Rita's batch and, anyway, she needn't marry a batchmate, or even a boy from the IAS at all.' Though he said so, he secretly knew he would love Rita to marry someone from the IAS. It all became much more convenient. But he had to admit that nowadays too few Sikh boys were competing for and qualifying for the IAS. They were, like his son, either into some business of their own or looking to emigrate abroad—if they were not already into drugs, that is.

'I told you, Mamma, it is of no use trying to make him understand. I had known it all along.' Rita was desperately trying to keep up a brave face, to not let her emotions get the better of her. It was not only the cruelty and insensitivity of it all but the sense of disappointment that she felt at her father's response, who had always loved her so much since she was a baby in his arms and had never denied her anything.

'Papa, I think Rita is right. It is her life, and times are changing. It would be in the fitness of things for us to give her our blessings and wish her the very best.' It was Baldev who now spoke. He was a man of few words but also a man of deep convictions, just like his father. It just happened that on the issue of Rita's choice of partner, Baldev's convictions were diametrically opposite to those of his father.

'I may have retired but this house is still mine, and though times have indeed changed, they have not changed so much that I now have to understand what is in "the fitness of things" from my children. It is her life alright, but it is my house.' Unreasonableness and defiance were carved on every feature of the old man's face. The words had been uttered, not in a fit of uncontrolled rage but with a deliberateness that accentuated the finality and brutality of his decision.

There was nothing left to be said—there was nothing that could possibly have been said that would have made the slightest difference to Tejveer Singh.

However, contrary to their fears, the situation had not turned ugly or messy. Perhaps Rita's father, the distinguished-looking ex-bureaucrat, hadn't lost his cool because of Rahul's quiet, confident demeanour or perhaps it had been his son's unexpected resistance and visible disagreement with his views. Though more than a little taken aback by the sudden appearance of his daughter, accompanied by a stranger, in his drawing room that evening, Tejveer Singh, despite his outward civility, remained adamant.

But if Rita's father was surprised at Rahul's temerity in showing up at his home to ask for his only daughter's hand in marriage, Rahul himself was shocked at finding the strength and courage to do so. Clearly, his love for Rita had brought out qualities in him that he never knew existed.

For Rita, it was not only a matter of her life, love and choice but also that of not succumbing to something she knew was wrong, a quality that had been ingrained in her by the very same upbringing her father had provided her. Her father hadn't anticipated that Rita would be prepared to live her life, independent of him, on her own terms.

As soon as the Chandigarh Express came to a stop at the Charbagh station next morning and Rita stepped out on the platform, greeted by her personal staff that had come to receive their 'respected madam', she started thinking of the next possible steps for them. She had always known that despite her pleadings, her father would say no to their marriage, but she somehow had more faith on Rahul's middle-class parents, from what she had seen of them that first day she had met them on the terrace. So it was the very next day of their arrival from Chandigarh that Rita insisted on going ahead and talking to Rahul's parents.

The sun had already set by the time Rahul and Rita reached his modest home that evening. All of them were sitting in the drawing-cum-living room. There was an old TV set in one corner and an even older sofa in the middle of the mid-size room. Though Rahul had always been distant and sometimes even uncomfortable with his father, that evening he was filled with a strange sense of assurance and confidence when addressing him.

'Papa, I had told you that I was going with Rita to Chandigarh for a break, but what I didn't tell you was that we had gone to meet Rita's father and ask him for his consent to our marriage.'

This piece of news must have been a shock to his poor parents, Rahul thought, but they didn't let it show. They were probably more eager to hear what had happened next. This time it was Rita who spoke.

'Unfortunately, I couldn't convince my father to give his consent and blessings to our proposed marriage. It had nothing to do with Rahul—it's just that my family is very orthodox and can't seem to agree to an inter-faith, inter-state, inter-caste marriage.'

For Rahul's parents, the revelations were too many, too fast. The news of their only son having fallen in love with his batchmate, going all the way to Chandigarh without their knowledge to try and convince the girl's parents on his own, his failure to do so and the predicament that he now faced, all struck Mr and Mrs Srivastava one after the other. Their full import was yet to sink in, when Rita spoke once again about their plans.

'We will have to go for a court marriage. I have never liked the band, baaja, baraat type anyway, although my father would have loved it. But given the circumstances, it will be the most sensible thing to do.'

'We would love you both to be there with us, in our decision and in our course of action. It is the very same request we made to her parents in Chandigarh. Though we were not successful there, we hope you will give us your blessings.' Rahul looked straight at his parents, from one to the other, with a mix of hope, faith and defiance. He was aware that he had put them in an uncomfortable position, especially in front of Rita, but there seemed to be no other way.

Mr Srivastava looked at his wife, and after the silent, brief look of understanding from her he had grown used to in the past 25 years, proceeded to speak.

'We would love to welcome Rita in our humble abode and in our family, though our circumstances and lifestyle are not something she is used to. But Rita's parents' refusal to agree to your marriage makes me uncomfortable. If you two are thinking of getting married without their consent, it might bring about an unbridgeable gap between Rita and her parents. Can she really live her life happily without their love and support? Perhaps we should wait and try to convince them again.'

Though Mr Srivastava wanted to see his only son happy, felt for this girl sitting opposite him and would have been happy and proud to see them married, he still feared the consequences of Rita's defiance of her father's wishes and the unpleasantness it would inevitably generate. Moreover, he feared that he would be blamed for encouraging the defiance, of conspiring behind Rita's parents' back in arranging this marriage.

'No, Uncle, that won't be wise, I am afraid. I know my father but I know myself and my mind too.' It was Rita once again. 'We plan to meet the marriage officer soon and do the formalities of public notice, etc. After the required period of one month, we will go for a simple court marriage. That day, of course, we would like you to be there.'

'That is alright, but we, too, have our relations and friends, and Rahul is our only son. We will have to organise a proper function and invite our guests. They will be expecting that, and even we would like that very much.' It was the first time that Mrs Srivastava had spoken that evening but her tone was decisive.

'Yes, of course, that can very well be arranged.' Rahul realized that Rita would perhaps feel uncomfortable in formal functions where her own parents were not present, but he felt it was impossible not to accede to his mother's simple wish of celebrating her only son's wedding. His feelings of a vague sense of guilt in concealing his feelings and intentions from his parents for so long had slowly dissolved into one of unspoken thankfulness and relief. In a way, he felt vindicated in having faith in his parents and to find them so much more liberal, open and loving than Rita's. It gave him a sense of pride and contentment that was hard to articulate, and he realized that day just how much their consent mattered to him.

Feroze had presumed that Mr Athawale's story would be about a scam or a wrongdoing involving some of his departmental colleagues or superiors with whom he had some axe to grind. But as soon as Mr Athawale started talking, Feroze realized he had grossly underestimated the man's acumen and abilities.

'You know, Feroze sa'ab, I heard you making those enquiries about pollution in the Gomti River the other day at Mr Rathee's office and thought you would be interested in knowing what I have to tell you.' It was once again a painful reminder to Feroze that his story on the Gomti's pollution caused by Lucknow Distilleries hadn't seen the light of day. Feroze had ordered a cappuccino for himself and Mr Athawale a bun-maska and chai.

'You will probably remember that about a year or so ago, Lucknow Distilleries came up with a dedicated effluent treatment plant. It was inaugurated by the Chief Minister, and the owners and managers had claimed that it was the most modern and sophisticated effluent treatment plant in India.' Mr Athawale was clearly warming up to his story. Feroze had covered the inauguration for his newspaper and remembered it quite clearly. He remembered feeling a secret vindication that it was his story, no matter if it had been killed, and the possibility that another such story could surface again, that had forced the distillery owners to commission the effluent treatment plant. He had secretly congratulated himself that the Gomti would now breathe easier.

'Since the inauguration, Mr Rathee says that the effluent discharge of Lucknow Distilleries is virtually pollution-free and that the quality of water has shown remarkable improvement. I believe he has even shared the data with you.' Mr Athawale continued.

Feroze couldn't really understand where the conversation was leading. What Mr Athawale was telling him was public knowledge and had nothing to do with either him or the electricity department. But his next statement immediately showed Feroze once again how wrong he had been in his estimation of this small, diminutive-looking junior engineer who sat opposite him, chomping away on his bun-maska and relishing the hot tea in front of him.

'But you know what, Feroze sa'ab, in the past few months, the electricity bill of the distillery has not gone up at all! Effluent treatment plants are electricity guzzlers, no matter how modern and sophisticated they are, so clearly, something is funny here. The distillery is running at full capacity, the effluent treatment plant has come up, the pollution levels are down—and yet the electricity bills have not increased at all!' Mr Athawale was now looking directly at Feroze through his thick, dark-rimmed spectacles. Both men were now equally focussed on the conversation, oblivious to the beauty of the Himalayas around. Feroze's mind was already working overtime, trying to connect the dots, but he decided to take things one at a time, as Mr Ghosh had taught him to.

'Can you give me the copies of their electricity bills over the past few months—from before the time the effluent treatment plant came up to later—those that show that there has been no increase in electricity consumption ever since the effluent treatment plant was commissioned?' Feroze knew he needed documents to back up any story he might have and wanted to get his hands on them as soon as possible.

'Yes, of course. Obviously I am not carrying them here with me but I will get them delivered to your office when I return to Lucknow on Tuesday.'

'Please, get them delivered at our reception in a sealed envelope, clearly marking it for me. Don't write your name on it or give any indication of what it contains.' Feroze knew that this was 'big', far bigger than what Mr Athawale suspected or imagined. He was sure Mr Athawale had no clue about who the real owner of Lucknow Distilleries was. Feroze was also sure that if Mr Athawale knew it was Sheshmani Pandey, nephew of the Chief Minister and virtual No 2 of the state ruling party, he would have refrained from sharing his knowledge with Feroze. In fact, he wondered what had made Mr Athawale so keen to share his story with him.

'Why are you telling me all this? For all you know, the effluent treatment plant may be working fine and they may be indulging in electricity theft by bypassing the meter or something. In that case, it is your department that should be investigating. After all, such things happen all the time.' Feroze knew and was sure even Mr Athawale knew that that was a very real possibility.

'I also thought so and wanted to investigate, but those fellows would just not let me enter their premises! When I insisted, I got so many phone calls and threats that I finally had to give up. It was really rather unusual, as if they had paid everybody to cover things up.' Mr Athawale continued. 'Those bastards at Lucknow Distilleries think they are too big.'

Now Feroze could, for the first time, get a glimpse of what lay behind Mr Athawale's deep resentment of the distillery, but he decided to suspend, at least for the time being, any judgement on Mr Athawale's motives. To him, the story and its possible consequences mattered; Mr Athawale's motives were secondary. Feroze wanted to interject and tell Mr Athawale that a suspected case of electricity theft was not really a story for a national-level newspaper but before he could say anything, Mr Athawale continued.

'I didn't give up, though. I put up a second check meter on the transformer outside their premises. They couldn't stop me from doing that, since it was outside their premises and our department was already putting up such check meters for all large consumers. I personally checked the readings and am pretty sure there is no electricity theft there. In that case, there can be only one conclusion—the effluent treatment plant is simply not working!'

'And yet the discharge to the Gomti, as Mr Rathee's test report shows, is remarkably pollution-free.' Feroze completed the statement. There was clearly something amiss here, something sinister and fishy.

'Ok, Feroze sa'ab, I will send the electricity bills to your office as soon as I return to Lucknow. I think those bastards are up to something. Since you already seemed to be curious about something of that sort when I saw you in Mr Rathee's office, I decided to tell you this.' Clearly, Mr Athawale was bringing their conversation to a close and was looking at his wristwatch. Perhaps, Feroze surmised, he had promised his family he would rejoin them at a particular time. After all, Mr Athawale had come to Simla on holiday and it was by sheer chance that he had bumped into Feroze that morning.

Feroze asked for the bill but Mr Athawale insisted on paying for both of them, as Feroze had half-expected.

As they climbed down the rickety wooden staircase of the café and stepped out on to Mall Road, Feroze could see that it had changed in the past one hour. The sleepy, beautiful, colonial road was now bursting at the seams with tourists, local officegoers, students, loafers, labourers and honking vehicles. Feroze bid Mr Athawale goodbye and started walking towards the greener and salubrious environs of the erstwhile viceregal lodge. He hoped that by that time, Sharmila would have been done with her conference and her academic work and would have got free for the day.

He hoped that for the next two days, they would be able to enjoy their togetherness and intimacy in the quiet Himalayan landscape—exclusive, precious and ultimately hopeless.

It had been some time since Dinesh, Feroze and Rahul had met up at Moti Mahal, their old Hazratganj haunt. In recent years, a number of new cafés and restaurants had opened up in Gomti Nagar, especially in the areas near the Patrakarpuram, and slowly but inexorably the heart of the Lucknow dining and entertainment scene had moved from Hazratganj of Kwality, Royal Café and Moti Mahal to Gomti Nagar of Vintage Machine and Mocha Café. But still, the three friends had decided on Moti Mahal that Sunday afternoon. Actually, it had been Feroze's idea, as it was he who had rung the other two up, asking them to meet him. It was rather unusual for Feroze, thought Rahul, to take the initiative. Even in the good old days of their leisurely youth, it was never Feroze who had taken the initiative. At that time, Rahul thought, it must have been Feroze's strained finances that would have stopped him.

Apparently, Dinesh had also suspected that something was up that had prompted Feroze, with all his work engagements, studies and Ms Basu, to arrange for this impromptu meeting.

'So, what's up? From your voice on the phone, it appeared that you wanted to discuss something important and big.' Dinesh was right. Even Rahul had sensed the barely concealed excitement in his friend's voice when he had called up at Barabanki that morning. Feroze had even asked Rahul to request Rita to come. Rita had promised she would but said she first had some law and order duty to take care of.

'Yes. It is about a story on which I wanted your advice and possible help.' Feroze started explaining, but only after the three friends had ordered their samosas and bun-maskas with tea.

'I have the masala but not the evidence to pin it down. About a year back I had written a story on how Lucknow Distilleries was pumping untreated, polluted effluent directly into the Gomti daily.'

'I don't remember reading anything of that sort.' Rahul was sure, because he eagerly and regularly read any story with Feroze's byline.

'That's because it never appeared in print. It was the only time I, or rather my editor—whom I respect very much otherwise—had to compromise and, under huge pressure from our owners, refrain from breaking the news.' Feroze told them about the aborted story.

Though Dinesh was not surprised at the suppression of editorial and journalistic freedom, he was curious to know who owned Lucknow Distilleries. He remembered he had read somewhere that the original owners, who had founded the distillery about half a century back, had sold their stakes.

'My editor did tell me that the phone had gone straight from the Chief Minister's office to our managing director. I found out that it is Sheshmani Pandey who owns the majority share of the distillery and is its ultimate boss, although he goes to great lengths to keep it under wraps.' Feroze went on.

'That is quite understandable, but what has turned up now? What you just said concerns something that happened almost a year back. At that time, you didn't tell us anything.' It was Dinesh. Probably Feroze didn't appreciate fully the latent rivalry that existed between Dinesh and Sheshmani within the ruling party; perhaps Feroze even suspected that Dinesh, being a member of the ruling party, a legislator and son of a former Cabinet minister, would feel uncomfortable about Feroze's breaking such a damaging story connected to Sheshmani, and by extension, the Chief Minister himself.

'Anyway, the distillery set up a modern effluent treatment plant on its premises, which was inaugurated by the Chief Minister himself.' This was something that both Dinesh and Rahul remembered. 'The pollution level of the effluent that the distillery is now discharging into the Gomti has gone down dramatically since then.' Feroze added.

'So what is the story now?' Rahul was getting a little impatient. Rita was getting late and, unknown to both Feroze and Dinesh, they, too, had something to share with them that Sunday afternoon—something that was, at least to him, far more momentous than anything Feroze might have to say.

'I have found from their electricity bills, right from before the effluent treatment plant was commissioned to later, and their excise-duty data, that though the distillery is working at full capacity, the effluent treatment plant is definitely not. Now this, coupled with the fact that the groundwater in the Chowk area—which residents are pumping up for drinking—has shown the presence of similar pollutants that were initially found in the effluents before the treatment plant was commissioned, clearly point to the fact that Lucknow Distilleries is directly pumping its polluted discharge underground. That is what is causing the entire groundwater of the old city to get dangerously polluted; people are drinking this groundwater and that is what is causing the mysterious mini-epidemics there!' Feroze blurted out, excited and breathless.

Just then, Rita entered the dark environs of the restaurant from the glare of the afternoon sun and, greeting them with her usual effervescent smile, took up the fourth chair. Apparently, she had gone first to her recently acquired government quarters to take a quick shower before coming to meet them. So that was what had kept her so long, Rahul thought. But as she sat down and the subtle fragrance emanating from her filled his senses, he was glad that Rita was finally there, even if she had kept them waiting. Only Rahul could understand, even if not in full measure, what emotional turmoil she must be going through, having cut herself off from her family and parents for the sake of her love, freedom and Rahul.

'So what is stopping you from making a big story out of it? It is definitely a front-page, all-edition story, with the spotlight on public health. More importantly, Sheshmani owns the distillery. Now don't tell me that your editor and owner are again buckling down.' Dinesh could sense that it was big, and he, unlike the others, knew how big it could be for his own political future and how this one scandal could stop in its tracks Sheshmani's ascent to the top.

'I have not shared the story with my editor yet.' Feroze didn't tell his friends that he had already talked the story over in greater detail with Sharmila, on their return journey from Chandigarh and that it was on her suggestion that he had decided to talk things over with Rahul and Feroze. In fact, it was Sharmila who had suggested involving Rita, as it was in her administrative jurisdiction that Lucknow Distilleries was located. 'I have circumstantial evidence, not direct proof that the distillery is pumping its pollutants underground—no photographs, no witnesses, no official documents. No credible newspaper, even without any pressure or complicity, is going to print it.'

It had taken only a few minutes for Rahul to fill Rita in on what Feroze had told them so far, and she had not only understood the story but even warmed up to it.

'Look, it is in my subdivision. My officials and I can go to the distillery's premises on some innocuous pretext—labour survey, safety inspection, that sort of thing—and then get photographs of the pumping equipment.'

Rahul, the mechanical engineer that he was by education, had to interject. 'And there has to be a qualified engineer with you who understands these things and can point to the right pumps, as from outside, it is difficult to differentiate them from the normal ones that pump up underground water for other purposes.'

'I know someone in the Pollution Control Board, an engineering consultant, one Mr Khan. He is a young chap, utterly selfless, fearless and good at his job. You can take him along. I will brief him.' Dinesh interjected. 'But won't your editor succumb like last time?' Dinesh now turned to look at Feroze.

'We will see to that when the time comes, but, believe me, in today's age, without creating headlines, law enforcement is near impossible, even if there are incorruptible officers,' Feroze said thoughtfully.

'That might be so, but Feroze, as a magistrate on duty, I can give you a window of 15 days to break your story. But once I see that the story has been killed, I, on my own, will have to go ahead and take legal action, whatever the consequences.' Rita, the fun-loving, gregarious girl was now all quiet certitude and grim determination.

It had been this tenacious fearlessness and strict adherence to her moral compass that had attracted Rahul to Rita in the first place. This was what had made Rita different from the others in the academy, Rahul realized with pride. He thought it was time to announce his own plans, rather theirs, to his boyhood friends, now that Feroze's course of action had almost been finalized.

It was well past 7 p.m. but there was still a mountain of files in front of Suresh Kumar. It had almost been two months since he had been Chief Secretary of Uttar Pradesh and was only slowly getting used to the heavy load of the position. He remembered that, in comparison, the workload in his previous assignment as Secretary to the Government of India had been much less—by this time he would have been enjoying his daily evening walk with his wife in the leafy compound of the New Moti Bagh Colony.

But there was not too much time to reminisce, as his young, enthusiastic staff officer started explaining the next file from his 'dummy' notesheet. It was a particularly complicated issue concerning a personnel's court case and Kumar needed to concentrate but, irritatingly, the telephone next to his desk rang. He had given standard instructions to his staff to not transfer any calls at this hour, except those from the Chief Minister's or the Prime Minister's office. So he was quite surprised when his secretary revealed that it was Sardar Tejveer Singh, retired chief secretary of Punjab and his old boss in the Government of

India, who was on the line. Kumar knew his old boss had a way of breaking through the pitiful barriers of excuse his personal staff would have put up. He didn't blame them that they had felt it more prudent to transfer the call rather than subject themselves to the retired officer's wrath. But he wondered what had prompted his old boss to call him up. He remembered that Tejveer Singh's daughter had recently joined the UP cadre as a young subdivisional magistrate.

'Hi, Suresh, I am sure you are keeping awfully busy and must be doing a stupendous job too. I know what it takes to be a chief secretary, believe me.' It was the same old, confident man he remembered. He wondered when he would come to the point. As soon as Kumar had learnt that Rita was Tejveer Singh's daughter, he had made sure she had been posted in Lucknow district, not out of any great regard or affection for his old boss but from the mere knowledge that the retired officer, out of a sense of entitlement, would be expecting him to.

'Perhaps you know, Suresh, that my daughter, my only daughter, Rita, is now in service in the UP cadre. Of course, I never mentioned this to you earlier, as there was no reason to and I wanted my little girl to chart her own career.' Tejveer Singh continued. 'But I find that she has been posted in the state capital itself. Now I don't know whether you took the decision or if it was merely by chance, but I fear that she will have too much of a comfortable life in Lucknow and won't get to do a real SDO's job in a remote mofussil area, as we all did. I remember my good old days, and can still vouch for the importance of roughing it out in the initial years. So what I would want is for her to be posted to a remote district, as far away from Lucknow as possible, as soon as possible. Beyond that, it is entirely your choice where you post her—to the Bihar border or to Bundelkhand or wherever—but as far away as possible from Lucknow. Please do it and let me know.'

The last sentence had the sound of an order, which Kumar didn't like. It was as if the old Sardar still believed that he was Kumar's boss. Kumar didn't like remembering those days, not too distant either, when Tejveer Singh, then secretary to the Government of India, used to speak to him in a similar tone. Kumar had resented his boss's intolerant behaviour, his sense of entitlement and unjustified arrogance even then, but had decided to keep quiet and let things be. He decided once again to not rake up an issue.

'Ok, sir. I will see what I can do. Be assured of that.' For the first time in his life it was Suresh Kumar who disconnected the call with Tejveer Singh. He remembered all those days that he had tolerated his boss's snide comments and sarcastic remarks, only to maintain a clean annual confidential report, which he needed for his next promotion. He had managed to get that elusive promotion later but could never overcome his latent hatred for his boss.

'I wonder why he wants his daughter to be posted out. He was my boss once and I know him enough to understand that the reason he just threw at me is pure bullshit.' Kumar said out loud and looked at his young staff officer, only half expecting an answer. But Vinay Patwardhan, his staff officer, was better informed and had a ready explanation to offer.

'Sir, you might have heard that Rita, the SDM Lucknow you just spoke of, is going around with a batchmate of hers—

one Rahul Srivastava. Rahul is posted in Barabanki and is a Lucknow boy. In fact, only a few days back, the two have given notice of their marriage at the court of the ADM, Lucknow. Although Dinesh Singh, the young MLA and son of the former revenue minister, and a few others were witnesses, the news did not make it to the local papers. I believe Rahul's friend from the media—a chap called Feroze, who was also one of the witnesses—had a role to play in that.'

Kumar had no idea about these things but now that Vinay told him the facts, the real reason behind Tejveer Singh's call became clear. Kumar was not sure if his old boss was aware of the court marriage notice but knew that the man had definitely tried to block the proposed matrimony and now wanted the two lovers separated, possibly permanently. Kumar still remembered the old man's ossified prejudices and narrow-mindedness from the days they had shared the same floor in Shastri Bhawan.

'Sir, will you post her out? You know you would have to send a formal request to the Election Commission in that case, as the work of the voter list revision is currently on and the transfer of officers involved in the exercise is temporarily banned.' Kumar knew that Vinay was always well informed and exceptionally thorough in such issues. That is why he had been so highly recommended for the post of his staff officer when Kumar had rejoined the state cadre after a gap of almost six years. He had to admit that Vinay had never disappointed him.

'Of course not. It's none of my business to go playing the spoiler in two young people's love lives. In fact, we should invite the couple over for tea one of these days and wish them luck.' Apart from defying Sardar Tejveer Singh, Kumar genuinely felt for the young couple. He remembered how he himself had not been able to marry that Christian northeastern girl from his Mussoorie Academy days because of the combined opposition from both their families. Even after more than three decades, Kumar had not been able to forget Josephine.

Rahul had been able to convince Rita that she should not personally lead the survey team to Lucknow Distilleries and instead, delegate it to her trusted naib-tehsildar Mr Anjore, who would be accompanied by Mr Khan, the engineer Dinesh had recommended from the Pollution Control Board. Apart from the protective instincts that Rahul had recently developed for Rita, much to the latter's amusement, it made sense. An SDM—that, too, a glamorous lady officer such as Rita—leading a mere survey team to the distillery would raise suspicions in the minds of the distillery management. Further, he was sure that Sheshmani would notice that Feroze and Dinesh had both accompanied Rahul and Rita for their court marriage proceedings a few days ago.

The result of Mr Anjore's 'expedition' was much more successful than they had imagined. They had been able to get clear photographs of the pumps, which were undeniably pumping polluted discharge directly underground. Although all three friends had shared and kept copies of the castigating evidence that was enough to nail Lucknow Distilleries—and by extension Sheshmani Pandey—it naturally fell on Feroze to collate the evidence into a cogent and hard-hitting story.

Feroze had spent the better part of two days and two nights writing and rewriting his story, weaving in the evidence—tax returns, electricity bills, pollution levels in both the Gomti River and the groundwater, photographs of the patients at the medical college and lastly, but most importantly, the photographs of the pumps inside Lucknow Distilleries that were directly pumping pollutants underground. He was satisfied and silently proud of the final product, but as he handed over his story to Mr Ghosh that morning, he found himself holding his breath in anticipation of his editor's reaction. He wondered what he, Feroze, would do if once again his story was 'killed'—whether he would put in his papers in protest, whether he would even be brave enough to risk unemployment for the sake of his professional integrity when his family was so dependent on his salary. With his fears, pride and future in suspended animation, Feroze waited for Mr Ghosh's reaction, as the editor finished reading the story, put down the manuscript on the table, faced Feroze and looked at him over his reading glasses.

'Feroze, I am really proud of you. This is what is called 'real' news—real investigative journalism in today's age of feel-good news and government promotions masquerading as news. It touches human lives and aims to expose a deadly wrong, has big political repercussions and is fully covered with credible and undeniable evidence.' Mr Ghosh started but something in his voice and manner of speaking suggested to Feroze that there was a catch.

'Let me be honest, Feroze, and tell you that with the present ownership of this "hallowed" newspaper, there is no way this story is going to appear in print. If it does, we know we will both be sacked. But tell me, do you want this story to appear in print or do you want this story to appear under your name and under this newspaper's banner?'

Feroze hadn't anticipated this question and it took him a while to understand the true purport of Mr Ghosh's query.

'It is a big story, sir, and I would naturally like it to appear with my byline; but if it is really impossible, as you say, I am ready to compromise as long as the story breaks in a credible newspaper with a large-enough readership.'

'That is such a relief, Feroze, because if you had said no, frankly, we both would have had to put in our papers. I know your family situation and I, too, have a teenage daughter whose studies I have to support. But I promise you that this news is going to hit even bigger, bigger than you can imagine right now.' Mr Ghosh's mind was already moving ahead to the marriage reception his old boss was throwing at Delhi Press Club that evening. His old boss of a reputed Calcutta daily, a revered and fearless owner and editor, was a man of the old block who had been of late categorised as a sort of 'freak' case by the mainstream media. Mr Ghosh knew that if anybody could break this story, it was Mr Delmore. Feroze's story would indeed hit the ceiling. Mr Ghosh was aware that unlike his own publication, Mr Delmore's group had already ventured into the new and exciting space of online media and that online and social media would magnify Feroze's story manifold. He felt sad that Feroze's story, which had taken guts and hard work, would appear under somebody else's byline in some other publication and the glory that was rightfully his would be conferred on some totally undeserving reporter, simply because the owner and editor of his newspaper didn't have the guts to unmask the truth.

It had actually been rather easy for Dinesh to get in touch with the national president of their party, Bhawani Pratap Singh. Perhaps the young president had heard about him from some other quarter or perhaps their only meeting in Lucknow had been so profusely captured by the photojournalists that it had left an impression on the young leader's mind. Whatever the reason, only a day after Dinesh had left a message at the office and residence of Bhawani Pratap in Delhi, he was pleasantly surprised to receive a call back. Dinesh wondered if it was normal etiquette at the office of the new national president, but somehow doubted it.

Dinesh was sitting with Amrita at the breakfast table in their government bungalow's drawing-cum-dining room when his mobile phone rang. Amrita, of course, could hear only one side of the conversation but that was enough for her to understand what was being said.

'Yes, sir. This is Dinesh.'

'Yes, the reason I called you was that I wanted to come and meet you in person in Delhi. It is both important and urgent.'

'No, I can't talk about it on the phone but it is concerned with an impending scam that may blow up in the face of the state unit, the state government and the party, by extension.'

'I have very good reason to fear that.'

'I just want that you know about this, so that you may be

able to take whatever preventive or evasive action you may think is necessary.'

'No, it has nothing to do with me.'

'I just feel the same loyalty to the party that my father did, where he served for so long.'

'Believe me, it is big, otherwise I wouldn't have bothered you at all.'

'Ok. Monday then. I will come to your residence at 9 in the morning.'

'It is done, then. Thank you. I will be there on time.'

Amrita was, of course, one of the very few who knew what scam Dinesh was referring to. When exactly it would break none of them knew, as Feroze had told them that the story had been handed over to a prestigious rival media group and that even he didn't know when and how—even whether—the news would break.

'Don't you think you are betraying the faith that Feroze and Rahul put in you? Do they know what you intend to do?' Amrita asked after some time, slowly, deliberately, as she was wont to do when she felt it was something important.

'I don't know. I not only feel for Feroze and Rahul but more for the young children whose health and lives are in danger. I am as surely going to put an end to this nefarious activity at Lucknow Distilleries as Rahul and Feroze would like to. But yes, I also feel a sense of loyalty to my party, even more to our father lying in bed in the other room, who gave his life's work to strengthen the party. I also really believe that if the party goes down, the country will descend into chaos or end up with people who are much more unscrupulous.' Dinesh answered.

He knew that he had spent a few restless, sleepless nights thinking about it and was sure that what he was doing was right. Sometimes, in life, the larger good of a larger number of people became more important. But he was not sure whether he would ever be able to reveal, let alone explain, this to Feroze and Rahul. He hoped that at least Amrita, his own blood, would understand. He had not even shared his plans with Geeta, at least, not yet.

'I just hope everything ends well, for all of you and for all the right people. It must have been a difficult decision, but then who would know that better than you? I don't know whether I could have taken it myself.' Amrita was at least not horrified at Dinesh's plan. She could easily have regarded it as opportunistic betrayal and felt outraged, but she didn't, and that was enough for Dinesh that Friday morning.

Dinesh hoped that his boyhood friends would be as charitable and understanding. He hoped Geeta would be too, because sooner or later she would learn about this and what she thought mattered to Dinesh, as much, and perhaps more, than what anyone else did.

The Lucknow Mail had been late that morning and Dinesh could just about manage a quick shower and a cup of tea at the UP Bhawan at Sardar Patel Marg in New Delhi before starting for the residence of Bhawani Pratap Singh. A year ago, Bhawani Pratap had moved with his family to a separate residence from the Prime Minister's official residence, where his father lived—

and had been living since he became prime minister almost a decade ago. The ostensible reason forwarded to the public had been that the all-pervading security apparatus of the Special Protection Group of the Prime Minister impinged on the free movement of public and party workers who wanted to meet the newly elected national president of the ruling party. Although there had been some media speculation about whether that indeed was the real reason, it had soon died down and, for all practical purposes, the father and son appeared to maintain a perfect relationship—functional and political.

As Dinesh's car moved through the green, immaculately maintained roads of central Delhi, with its roundabouts adorned with statues of leaders long forgotten, towards Aurangazeb Road, his Blackberry phone rang. It was Geeta.

'No, the story has not broken in the newspaper today but the publication has been releasing teasers on their online version since morning, hinting at a scandal that has been putting the lives and health of hundreds of people in danger and which involves a very important political family in Uttar Pradesh.'

Both Dinesh and Geeta had been wondering for the past couple of days whether the rival editor of Calcutta to whom Mr Ghosh had secretly handed over the story had also chickened out, or whether he had made a deal with Sheshmani, the Chief Minister, or even the powers in Delhi. The news was getting delayed and the deadline set by Rita was fast approaching. Dinesh was not entirely sure, with his mixed feelings and loyalties, whether he wanted the story to break, with its clearly negative political repercussions on his and his father's party. But he was, nevertheless, dead sure that he wanted the criminal activities at Lucknow Distilleries to stop immediately. He further wanted Sheshmani to not get any chance to capture the party apparatus and turn it into something nefarious, where people like Dinesh had no place.

But now, surely, the media publication of Calcutta was soon going to break the story, and break it big—otherwise they wouldn't have taken the trouble to put out the teasers on their online version. Suddenly, Dinesh understood why the clever editor had delayed breaking the story when he already had all the evidence and material in hand: the Parliament session had started that very day and he wanted the news to have the maximum impact, by making it 'the' issue the Opposition would latch on to.

All these thoughts were racing through Dinesh's mind as he was ushered into the sprawling government bungalow, past the rather non-invasive security, but not before having had to part with his mobile phone. If his getting an appointment with Bhawani Pratap with relative ease came as a surprise to Dinesh, the fact that he was asked to share breakfast with the second-most-powerful politician in the country was even more of a shock. He realized that in the political circles and circuses that he had seen till then, it was a privilege that many MLAs and ministers would gladly have given a fortune for.

Soon, a fresh-looking Bhawani Pratap, clad in crisp white kurta-pyjamas, entered the dining space, along with a waft of cologne, and took his seat. As the bearers got busy serving hot idlis and dosas, Bhawani Pratap, as was his nature, came straight to the point.

'So, the scandal that you were referring to on the phone, it appears, is coming to roost very soon. The *Calgraph Express* is posting teasers since morning on their online platform—I am sure it is the same that you wanted to talk about. Let me know what you know and what can be done. I am all ears.'

'Sir, there is an old distillery on the banks of the Gomti, called Lucknow Distilleries…' Dinesh had just started on his practised narrative and was taking out the supporting papers from his plastic folder, when he was interrupted.

'Please, don't call me sir. You can call me BP—it is what I prefer.'

It took a while for Dinesh to come to terms with this gesture of familiarity but he decided not to further use any address at all as he described in adequate detail the scandal, the criminal activities at Lucknow Distilleries and how the staff was deliberately pumping polluted discharge underground and putting the lives of residents in danger. He took care to explain how Sheshmani Pandey, the nephew of the Chief Minister and the de-facto leader of the state unit, owned and controlled the distillery and how the scandal, which could break out any day, had the power to destroy the reputation of Sheshmani, his uncle and, by extension, the party itself. The fact that in the media and in popular perception Sheshmani had painted himself as a recipient of Bhawani Pratap's blessings and as the heir apparent to the post of president of the state unit was deliberately pointed out by Dinesh, while appearing not too verbose. He knew Bhawani Pratap didn't have a longish attention span but saw that he had been successful in catching his attention and that his expression turned darker and stonier with every statement Dinesh uttered.

'The bastard, his greed and impunity would have taken us all down,' BP muttered. Dinesh picked up the subtle change in tense and the use of 'would have' instead of 'will'. Dinesh completed his side of the story and showed BP the documents he had, but was careful not to divulge how the scandalous story had reached the media or how Feroze, Rahul, Rita or anybody else was involved. He was relieved when he realized BP wasn't about to ask him for his source. He instead seemed to be thinking ahead furiously, trying to find ways and means to limit the inevitable damage. Almost even before Dinesh had ended his narrative, BP had connected to his father, the Prime Minister and the most powerful politician in the country.

Dinesh could hear the prodigal son explaining in short but clear sentences the scandal, the role of Sheshmani Pandey and the apparent damage it could cause the party, especially to the father-son duo. What Dinesh was more interested in was what action he would propose to his father.

'We have indeed escaped by the skin of our teeth. As you know, I was going to announce the name of Sheshmani Pandey as the new state president of Uttar Pradesh at the press conference this afternoon. The invitations are already out and although the press does not yet know the name, it is expecting an announcement, as we have already declared our "one man-one post" formula.'

'The news will definitely break tomorrow; we can't manage that damn editor. It is better to limit the damage.'

'If we announce somebody else—someone young, smart and clean, instead of the bastard Sheshmani—we can distance ourselves from him and his scandal.'

'It will give us an opportunity to get rid of him permanently. That bastard was using my name and gathering influence. He was getting too big for his boots.'

'Yes, I have somebody in mind. In fact, he is right now sitting in front of me.'

The last sentence struck Dinesh out of the blue and took him a while to understand what it exactly meant.

'The son of the comatose Surendra Singhji, the former Deputy Chief Minister who met with a near-fatal accident. If there has to be a change of guard, and there has to be one, I would much prefer him—no baggage, young, good-looking, eloquent and, most importantly, the right caste combination.'

'He will balance out our Brahmin Chief Minister. The Thakurs of eastern UP are getting restless.'

'Yes, I know he is young and inexperienced, but so was I. It is more of an advantage, rather than a disadvantage in today's age of scam-and-scandal-tainted politics, where all veterans are looked at with suspicion.'

'Of course, there are exceptions.'

Dinesh could easily make out the direction the conversation was taking and realized how that one telephone conversation was slowly but surely changing the direction of his own life, his coming years, his destiny and his future.

At just that moment Geeta and her face flashed in front of his eyes, her eyes sparkling and her smile impish. He realized that he could no longer think of a future without Geeta Zutshi. Whatever may be the uncertainties of his future as far as politics was concerned, Dinesh felt he had a rock of certainty with Geeta on his side. He was glad.

The lawns of the Civil Services Institute near the Governor House were decorated with strings of light. A famous tent house of Lucknow had set up shamianas of deep purple, gold and white with floral decorations. A massive arch had been installed at the entrance of the institute and soft, instrumental music was playing. Inside the shamiana, facing the sofas and chairs where the guests were supposed to sit, stood two identical throne-like chairs covered in red velvet for the bride and the groom. But Rahul and Rita were not sitting on them. Instead, they were moving around freely, smiling, chatting and mingling with the guests.

Though the court marriage had happened a couple of days ago at the Lucknow Collectorate, this time in the chambers of the District Magistrate, the day of reception had been chosen over the weekend. Unlike on the day of marriage, when only Rahul's parents, Dinesh, Amrita, Geeta and Feroze had been witnesses, today many officers of the cadre, including Suresh Kumar, Vinay Patwardhan and the respective bosses of the bride and the groom were also present. So also was Sardar Tejveer Singh.

Suresh Kumar liked to believe that it was his timely and gentle persuasion that had led his former boss to accept Rahul and Rita's marriage. It was typical of him to do so: throughout his life as a civil servant, and more so since he had assumed the role of chief secretary of the most populous state in the country, Suresh Kumar had thought that almost everything good or fortuitous that happened was influenced by him and his timely interventions.

But Rita, and to a smaller extent Rahul, realized that it was the sheer inevitability of events that had made the proud Sardar accept the situation. Whatever it was, the old man was clearly enjoying himself, with his wife and son in tow, meeting the more venerable guests and pretending as if the very idea of the wedding was his own. Suresh Kumar looked at his old boss and smiled.

There were some newspaper reporters and press photographers too, as not only was this one of the most talked-about and glamorous 'Page 3' marriages of the season, but also because Rita, the bride, had recently been all over the news with her actions in sealing Lucknow Distilleries and lodging an FIR against its management, including Sheshmani Pandey. Suresh Kumar remembered how, in the immediate aftermath of the stinking scandal hitting the roof, Rita had swung into action even before anybody could react. He remembered, too, how Sheshmani Pandey had stormed into his office demanding that the actions of the immature SDM be stopped immediately. But that the haughty politician had to actually walk into his office instead of making the Chief Minister call on his behalf, had been a sure indicator to the seasoned bureaucrat that the tide of fortune had turned. What Sheshmani had not known was that the Principal Secretary to the Prime Minister had forewarned Suresh Kumar of the events that would follow and had 'advised' him to let law take its course. That had meant that Suresh Kumar need not have done anything except sit and smile—something that he found quite easy to do.

Dinesh remembered that day when news of how the Gomti was being dangerously and deliberately polluted by Lucknow Distilleries had broken online. It was what the journalists would call 'the shit hitting the roof'. Every news channel and newspaper, friendly to the government or otherwise, had picked up the story and magnified it, some willingly, some uncertainly—but it was just too big to be ignored. But Bhawani Pratap and his father had played their cards well. Soon the bulletins were flooded with even bigger news—the party had appointed a clean, young face as the new president of the state unit of Uttar Pradesh. It was projected as a much-needed change of guard and of culture in the grand old party. Photographs of Dinesh and Bhawani Pratap sharing the dais and addressing the media had filled the front pages of newspapers the next day and pushed the story of Lucknow Distilleries to the bottom half. People in the know also saw that the party high command had distanced itself from Sheshmani Pandey, and his hangers-on, who used to crowd around him and his bungalow day and night, disappeared, only to resurface later in the state party headquarters professing a bright future for the party under the new state president.

Dinesh had witnessed this change in his fortunes and loyalties with mild amusement. He knew the people, the very few people who really mattered to him—Geeta, his father, Feroze, Rahul and Amrita—would always be there. He had been anxious only about how they would react to the fact that Dinesh had broken the news of the 'Gomti pollution scandal' to his party bosses without first taking them into confidence. But his faith in them and in the strength of their relationships had not been betrayed. They had understood his sense of loyalty to the party and that Dinesh's actions had only been aimed at salvaging his party's political fallout, not to cover up the scandal or shield the culprits. It was a relief for Dinesh to see that his relationships had not only withstood the scandal and its dramatic fallout but had also emerged stronger.

Dinesh had suggested that Rahul also invite the Chief Minister at his reception, but both Rahul and Rita had pointed out that neither did they know the CM personally, nor was the invite warranted. They didn't want to be seen as too close to any political power and feared that the arrival of the CM, with his entourage and security, would inconvenience the other guests. Dinesh had to agree that they had a point, although he knew that for his and Geeta's marriage, not inviting the CM was not an option. Different lives for different people, he surmised, as he and Geeta handed over the bouquet of pearl-white rajnigandhas to the beaming bride.

Rita was wearing a sari after a long time—a red silk Benarasi with golden brocade—and was looking especially resplendent. But so were Geeta and Amrita. The two friends were chatting away while enjoying their gol gappas a little distance away. Dinesh was glad to see his sister so happy. Amrita had been somewhat anxious when Dinesh had so suddenly been thrust into the post of the state party president, fearing the inevitable political intrigues, backbiting and the slow erosion of morals and ethics. But she had recovered, and had lately not only reconciled to the situation but was also happy seeing her brother get his much-deserved attention and enjoy his work in strengthening the party and helping the poor at the same time.

Although both Feroze and Ms Basu had been invited to the reception, Feroze had come accompanied only by his family, as Zaidi Saheb had known Mr Srivastava from the days when Feroze and Rahul went to the same school.

Despite Feroze's outward happiness, only he—and Sharmila—knew what was going on inside him. The good news that he had been selected as the sole correspondent of the *Calgraph Express* in Lucknow, something that not only gave Feroze a better salary and perks but made him an accredited journalist, had been more than tempered by the unexpected announcement that morning by Sharmila. She had applied for and been selected for a prestigious teaching and research assignment at the Indian Institute of Advanced Study in Simla and would be moving there in a few days. Feroze understood why Sharmila had kept this news from him. She was sure, and Feroze had to admit she was right, that if Feroze had known of her plans, he would have tried to opt as a special correspondent with his new firm at Chandigarh or even Simla. Feroze also knew that Sharmila didn't want him to be torn apart any longer by his conflicting loyalties to his family and his love for her. It was what was best for both of them, for all of them. Sharmila had told him that morning that they should move on with their lives and leave behind their brief relationship, beautifully hopeless as it was, just as a sweet, cherished memory.

Feroze knew that although she had been invited by both Rahul and Rita, Sharmila would not come. As Feroze looked around at the revelries and laughter, at the gaiety and decorations, at the pomp and pomposities, he felt he ought not to be so selfish and try to sincerely share in the joys of his childhood friends and their newfound loves. But Feroze knew his friends would see through his act, even if others didn't. Despite the happiness of his loved ones, Feroze felt something deep inside him crumbling, getting pulverised, as if a huge, dark void, an abyss, was opening up inside him, never to be filled again.

He had always known that Sharmila and he inhabited parallel

worlds. He had never given himself—or her—even the slightest hope that there could be a romantic possibility between them. But had he done the right thing? Would Sharmila have been wrong in expecting him to give her even the slightest indication that he wanted her? Yes, she had always known—but was that enough? The weight of all those years of silent attraction and yearning came crashing down on him as he saw Rahul and Rita climb up the low stage to their assigned seats, gently escorted by Rahul's mother. That could have been him and Sharmila. A sense of bitter remorse rose inside him as he thought about how, maybe, he had unknowingly pushed Sharmila away.

He squinted at the stage, trying to blink back the tears. Rahul and Rita looked perfect, the picture of happiness. He couldn't believe how far the three of them—Dinesh, Rahul and Feroze—had come since their days of Sunday cricket and jalopy outings. It was ironical how Dinesh's father's accident had actually led to father and son growing closer. What physical filial interaction could not achieve, the mere sight of his father on a hospital bed had. He knew part of Dinesh's frenzied political dedication was directed at making his father proud, though Raja Saheb may never be able to tell his son that.

Rahul's relationship with his father, too, had taken a happier turn. Where Rahul had felt claustrophobic at his father's tall expectations of him, now he felt gratitude. There was newfound respect, faith and love. Rahul had even told Feroze that he wanted to get the small, shabby kitchen renovated for his mother.

Despite himself, Feroze smiled. Different people, different lives. He could see his own parents and sisters standing near the stage, looking up with happy faces at the bride and groom. Feroze knew that although his father would have loved to see Feroze as an IAS officer like Rahul, he was happy that he had established himself so well and so quickly as a journalist. He tried to draw pride and comfort from that, and yet a paralysing sense of loneliness engulfed him.

The sound of train whistles that occasionally rose above the soft instrumental music reminded Feroze of that train journey on Chandigarh Express with Sharmila not so long ago. The happiness around only seemed to intensify Feroze's loss and he felt a gnawing chasm open up between him and everyone else—but, he realised with a lump in his throat, the only person who could help him fill it had disappeared, for ever out of his reach.